The Chicken for Every Occasion Cookbook

CONSUMERS UNION

Yonkers, New York

The Chicken for Every Occasion Cookbook

Helen Studley

and The Editors of Consumer Reports Books

Published by Consumers Union of U.S., Inc.,
Yonkers, New York 10703

Library of Congress Cataloging-in-Publication Data
Studley, Helen.
The chicken for every occasion cookbook.
Bibliography: p.
Includes index.
1. Cookery (Chicken) I. Consumer Reports Books.
II. Title.
TX750.5.C45S78 1988 641.6'65 88–71031
ISBN 0-89043-276-7
ISBN 0-89043-225-2 (pbk.)

Design by Joy Taylor

Drawings by Mona Mark

Fourth printing, August 1995
Manufactured in the United States of America

The Chicken for Every Occasion Cookbook is a Consumer Reports Book published by Consumers Union, the nonprofit organization that publishes *Consumer Reports*, the monthly magazine of test reports, product Ratings, and buying guidance. Established in 1936, Consumers Union is chartered under the Not-For-Profit Corporation Law of the State of New York.

The purposes of Consumers Union, as stated in its charter, are to provide consumers with information and counsel on consumer goods and services, to give information on all matters relating to the expenditure of the family income, and to initiate and to cooperate with individual and group efforts seeking to create and maintain decent living standards.

Consumers Union derives its income solely from the sale of *Consumer Reports* and other publications. In addition, expenses of occasional public service efforts may be met, in part, by nonrestrictive, noncommercial contributions, grants, and fees. Consumers Union accepts no advertising or product samples and is not beholden in any way to any commercial interest. Its Ratings and reports are solely for the use of the readers of its publications. Neither the Ratings nor the reports nor any Consumers Union publications, including this book, may be used in advertising or for any commercial purpose. Consumers Union will take all steps open to it to prevent such uses of its materials, its name, or the name of *Consumer Reports*.

To my husband

Contents

Acknowledgments

I would like to thank all who have helped me in the preparation of this book:

Nancy Love, my agent, for her trust, support, and encouragement along the way.
Julie Henderson, my editor, for her enthusiasm about the subject and for her editorial expertise.
Rick Steffan and Paolo Penati, chefs at our restaurant, for sharing their cooking skills with me and for putting up with my constant questions.
Florence Lin, for her down-to-earth advice and help on the Chinese dishes, and for her friendship.
Sean Giblin, owner of the Murray Hill Market in Sag Harbor, for telling me the basic facts about buying chicken.
Ira Barash, for his expert advice on how to carve a chicken.
Hilary Brown, of Consumers Union, for her recommendations on the handling of poultry.
Jonathan Waxman, Ellen Less, and Celeste Yazzetti, for the use of their recipes.
Hawa Diallo, Mercedes Sanchez Moreno, Maricel Prescilla, Julie Sahni, Diana Kennedy, Roberta Schneiderman, and Marie Sibony, for their valuable help on the ethnic cuisines.
And, finally, my friends and neighbors, for tasting a lot of chicken and thus doing their share in the making of this book.

The Chicken for Every Occasion Cookbook

Introduction

MY three-year-old grandniece, a highly discriminating diner, will try any dish once. Her rejection is swift; her acceptance conclusive. Her judgment is based on a single criterion: "Tastes like chicken." And, with that compliment, any food—be it herring, rhubarb, or summer squash—is permanently incorporated into her bill of fare.

Like my grandniece, I have always preferred chicken to other foods. Early on, I started to collect chicken recipes the way other people collect stamps, matchboxes, or miniature toys. Encountering a particularly good chicken dish in a restaurant, I would ask the chef for his recipe. Mention New Orleans, Marrakech, or New Delhi to me and I'll say: "Oh yes, that's where I tasted my first Cajun chicken, Mechoui, or Tikka Murgh."

One of chicken's most laudable attributes is the fact that it is high in protein and low in fat—a winning combination in today's age of nutritional enlightenment. It seems reasonable to me, then, not to smother the bird with heavy sauces, butter, and cream when preparing it. So the recipes in this book use modern cooking methods and low-fat ingredients. Steaming, slow stewing, poaching, broiling, or dry-sautéing are ideal ways of preserving the unique but subtle flavor of chicken;

good chicken stock, vegetable purées, and yogurt are ideal low-fat substitutes for flour and needless fats; fresh herbs and high-quality spices are imaginative flavoring agents that lead to exciting variations and, at the same time, all but eliminate the need for salt.

It is the ultimate tribute to chicken that, during all the time of testing, tasting, and developing recipes for this book, I never tired of the bird. The French, they say, have a different cheese for every day of the year. I would like to challenge them with chicken, one of the most versatile foods available today. This cookbook, I hope, proves my point.

A Word About . . .

Buying Chicken

In the course of testing over 300 chicken recipes for this book, I learned that a chicken is a chicken, but often can be a bird of a different color and flavor. The first roaster I cooked was tasteless, the second was juicy, the third was dry, and the fourth tough and stringy. Price had nothing to do with the finished product.

It helps to know that one week is the maximum to guarantee the freshness of a bird—that means seven days from the moment the chicken has been killed to the time it is cooked. The expiration date on packaged chicken refers to the shelf life of the bird, that is to say, from the day it has been cut up and packaged. It doesn't tell you how many days it has been kept in the store's refrigerator. If you add on the two days it takes for the chicken to reach the market, that packaged chicken may have been around for a week before it was labeled.

How should we shop for chicken? Go to the busiest supermarket in town because they move their products quickly. Stick to the same brand, which will help you become familiar with the product. Next look for a high-breasted bird, often an indication that the bird has received steady feeding and has had time to develop. Avoid buying chicken parts that are double-wrapped and have large amounts of blood in the package. Do not buy any birds that show traces of freezer burn, which means they have been stored for a long while. If, after all precautions, you find that the bird you bought has an unpleasant odor, do not cook it under any circumstances.

I would like to add one more bit of advice that I learned from the restaurant pros: Always examine the food you are buying. If it is not the freshest and best, don't buy it, or if necessary, return it. The quality of the meal depends on the quality of the ingredients.

Sanitary Handling of Poultry

Today's factory-bred chickens are particularly prone to contamination from salmonella, a group of bacteria that can cause food poisoning. Fortunately most, if not all, salmonella bacteria are killed during the cooking process. Most salmonella food poisoning comes from cross-contamination—bacteria from raw poultry left on the cutting board and utensils transfers to other foods—and multiplies rapidly in a warm kitchen.

Common sense prevails. Always wash whole chickens thoroughly inside and out before cooking, and pat dry (especially inside cavity). Wash chicken parts under running water, and pat dry. Always clean immediately, with hot soapy water, the sink, all utensils, and kitchen surfaces that have come in contact with the raw chicken. Wipe down wooden surfaces with a solution of bleach.

To store chicken, wrap the bird separately and cook it as soon as possible, or put it in the freezer for later use.

Heat alone is not sufficient to kill bacteria; the length of heating time is also vital. Since the heat inside the cooked stuffed bird is rarely hot for long enough to kill all bacteria, we recommend that you bake your stuffing separately and not inside the bird. Aside from health considerations, it is the opinion of some cooks (James Beard, for one) that stuffing tastes much better when cooked in a baking dish rather than inside the chicken—it's crispier, less soggy, and easier to serve. Try it.

If you do put stuffing into your roast chicken, add 45 minutes to 1 hour to the cooking time. Any stuffing mixture that requires cooking should always be cooked ahead of time and refrigerated. Remember, too, that the stuffing should be put into the bird only when you are ready to cook it. Do not pack it in too tightly; stuffing expands as it cooks. After the meal, remove the leftover stuffing from the chicken and refrigerate. Reheat it thoroughly before eating.

Oil

In this book I rarely specify which kind of oil to use because, with so many good oils around, choosing among them is a matter of personal taste. I have narrowed my choice down to olive oil, vegetable oil, and my own blend—a version of olive oil taught to me by a thrifty Italian housewife. The recipe follows.

Olive oil varies in character from country to country. The very best, from whatever country it originates, is extra-virgin oil, made from the first pressing of the olives. Intensely rich and flavorful, with a fruity aroma and rich texture, its color may range from golden yellow to dark green. Subsequent pressings produce olive oils with a less pronounced taste and paler color.

Generally, I use olive oil in those recipes where the oil's strong character enhances the flavor of the dish; occasionally, I may add a few drops of olive oil to a cooked dish to highlight its flavor or add an extra fillip of taste.

Vegetable oils are a blend of various vegetable products—soybean, cottonseed, grape seed, palm, and coconut oils. Light in texture, pale golden in color, their very blandness makes them ideal everyday cooking oils. When I sauté, I like to use a blend of two-thirds vegetable oil and one-third butter.

My Own Blend

8 ounces vegetable oil
8 green olives, pitted and crushed
4 cloves garlic, peeled and crushed

1. Pour the oil into an empty bottle; add the olives and garlic.
2. Close the bottle tightly, shake, and place in the refrigerator.
3. Shake bottle at least once or twice a week, and after four weeks you'll have a distinctly flavored oil. It approximates the taste of olive oil, without the heaviness. Keep in refrigerator or freezer, adding oil as needed and changing olives and garlic if desired.

Preparation

Planning a meal is as important as the actual cooking of the food. Preparation or, in cook's jargon, prepping, means the trimming, chopping, slicing, and necessary coordinating that precede the cooking.

In the classic French kitchen this process is called *mise en place*—loosely translated as "everything ready in place, done ahead of time." Each recipe in my book will give you the necessary preparation time required. In most instances the preparation may be done in advance, leaving you plenty of time to concentrate on the actual cooking of the dish.

How to Flambé

A flambé gives you the rich flavor of a cognac or liqueur in a dish without the sharp taste of the alcohol. To flambé safely and effectively, pour the required amount of liquor over the food in the pan, let it heat through, carefully toss a lit match on the surface, and immediately step aside. When the flames have died down, shake the pan back and forth to help prolong the burning process. Don't forget to retrieve the match. Do not flambé near curtains, pot holders, paper towels, or any other flammable fabrics.

Improvisation

Vatel, a celebrated French master cook during the reign of Louis XIV, killed himself before an important lunch because the specific fish he had ordered failed to arrive in time. Vatel missed the point: A good chef is supposed to be able to improvise.

Necessity is the mother of invention and, in the cooking world as elsewhere, this translates into imagination. If a called-for ingredient in these recipes is not available, go for an appropriate substitute. Some of the best dishes come about by accident.

Tools

Good tools are vital. Only a few items are needed, as long as they are kept at peak condition, carefully handled, and well looked after. Restaurant chefs guard their knives with their lives—small wonder, since good knives are their most important equipment, and represent a considerable investment.

Since we are only concerned with chicken, the following tools will do nicely:

Boning knife: 5 to 6 inches. The blade is slim and pointed and the handle is broad.
Chef's knife: 8 to 10 inches. This knife has a heavy triangular blade.
Carving knife: This knife has a long, curved blade.
Steel: Used for sharpening knives.
Tongs: Allow you to turn chicken pieces without piercing the skin.
Cleaver: Useful for chopping chicken parts and joints.
Poultry shears: Handy for cutting chicken parts cleanly and conveniently.

Guide to Cooking Methods

Roasting

Roasting, a dry-heat process, cooks the chicken evenly on all sides. There are two schools of thought about oven roasting. One favors roasting in a low-temperature oven, cooking the chicken at a constant temperature of 325° to 350°F. This method results in less shrinkage and is thought to make for a more tender bird. The other school prefers a high-temperature of 425° to 450°F. at the beginning of the cooking period, continuing at a lower temperature for the balance of the cooking time. This method helps to sear the surface of the bird, and helps retain its internal juices. Either way, always start by preheating your oven to the desired temperature before proceeding with roasting.

Personally, I prefer the latter roasting method, on which the following time chart is based. Since ovens vary and rarely register the correct temperature, a reliable oven thermometer is critical.

Set oven temperature at 450°F. Keep the maximum temperature for the first 15 minutes, then reduce the heat to 350°F. to complete cooking. Frequent basting will prevent the bird from becoming dry. Cooking time for an unfrozen, unstuffed bird is usually 20 minutes to the pound. But ovens vary, so use a meat thermometer if you wish. Insert it into the fleshiest part of the leg (avoid the bone), and take the chicken out of the oven when the thermometer registers 175°F. Another time-honored method: puncture the skin at the thigh joint. If the juices run clear, the chicken is done.

Ready-to-Cook Weight	*Approximate Cooking Time*	*Serves*
10-ounce squab	20 minutes	1
1¼- to 1½-pound Cornish game hen	30 minutes	2
2-pound chicken	50 to 60 minutes	3
3-pound chicken	1 hour and 10–20 minutes	4
4-pound chicken	1 hour and 15–30 minutes	4–5
4½-pound chicken	1 hour and 25–40 minutes	5–6
5-pound chicken	1 hour and 45 minutes	6–8

Trussing

To truss a bird may seem like a nuisance, but it is an important step in proper roasting. Trussing makes the chicken easier to handle, assures even cooking, and makes a more attractive presentation. Actually, trussing is as easy as bundling a baby; it takes longer to give exact directions than to do it. Although there are many ways to truss a bird, I prefer the following method, which produces a plumped-up breast, unmarked by the twine.

You will need a length of kitchen twine approximately 4 to 5 times the length of the chicken.

1. Stand the bird on its end, breast toward you, and grab the neck bone. Wrap the center of the twine around the neck bone. The twine is now in back of the chicken.

2. Lay the chicken on its back, and bring the twine toward the tail end of the bird. Bring twine forward, and cross over the ankles, pulling twine tight.

3. Bring twine up toward wing joint and flip the bird over.

4. Cross the twine over wings, pull tight, and tie securely. Cut off excess twine.

5. Tuck wings under twine to secure.

Broiling

Broiling, a method of cooking by direct, intense heat, is particularly well suited to cooking smaller pieces of chicken. Arrange the chicken parts on a flat pan and place under the broiler, about 3 to 4 inches from the heat. Broil 6 to 8 minutes on each side to sear. Total cooking time will vary according to the amount of heat and the size of the individual pieces. Check for doneness by piercing the thickest part of the meat with a fork or the tip of a sharp knife—the juices should run clear.

Grilling

Grilling or barbecuing can be done with either top or bottom open heat. Grilling over charcoal or over mesquite lends a characteristic taste to chicken. The process is quick and no added fat is necessary. Be sure to turn the meat frequently to avoid burning.

Timetable for Grilling

Parts	
Wings	12–14 minutes both sides
White meat	18–20 minutes both sides
Dark meat	25–30 minutes both sides
Halves	Grill, skin side down, for 5 minutes, then cook covered, skin side up, for 35–40 minutes
Whole (3½ pounds)	About 1½ hours in a covered grill, 1½–2 hours on rotisserie

A whole chicken can be cooked over indirect heat in a covered cooker, in which the heat is evenly distributed as it is in a convection oven. Arrange coals around a drip pan on the bottom of the grill. Place the chicken in the center of the cooking grid, directly over the drip pan.

Another excellent way to grill a whole chicken is on a rotisserie, where the rod acts as an additional heat conductor. Truss the bird by tying wings and legs securely to the body, then run the spit from neck to tail. Several birds can be grilled on the same spit by butting them neck to tail. It is a good idea to stuff the bird with onion, fruit, or parsley, which will help keep the bird moist while also adding flavor.

Steaming and Poaching

Steaming is cooking in the vapor arising from a boiling liquid. This method allows the chicken to retain its shape, color, and natural flavor. For steaming, a special steamer pan or a bamboo steamer may be used. In a pinch, you can create your own steamer by using a plain vegetable steamer basket placed over boiling liquid in a large pot. Whatever container you use, the steamer should be closely covered during cooking. (Be sure to save the remaining liquid for stock and future sauces.)

Poaching is one of the simplest ways to cook a chicken. If desired, you can blanch the whole bird first by immersing the chicken in boiling water for 1 to 2 minutes. Many cooks think blanching "tightens" the meat, rendering it juicier and more flavorful. Once the bird has been blanched, rinse it under cold water and place it in the hot liquid or broth to cover. Simmer for 20 to 30 minutes, skimming off any accumulated scum that rises to the surface. Turn off the heat and let it stand, tightly covered, for another 20 minutes, or until it is cooked. Poached chicken is particularly good for salads, since the meat will be flavorful and moist.

Sautéing

Sautéing is the method used for browning chicken parts in a skillet with a small amount of fat. If you use a nonstick pan, sautéing may be done without any fat. In order to sauté properly, preheat the skillet and fat before adding the chicken pieces.

Stewing

Stewing or braising is a slow method of cooking chicken parts in a tightly covered heavy casserole or Dutch oven, to which some liquid and vegetables have been added. For best results start off with an initial quick sauté to sear the meat. Cooking may then be done either on top of the stove over a low flame, or in a low-temperature oven of about 300°F.

Guide to Boning and Carving a Chicken

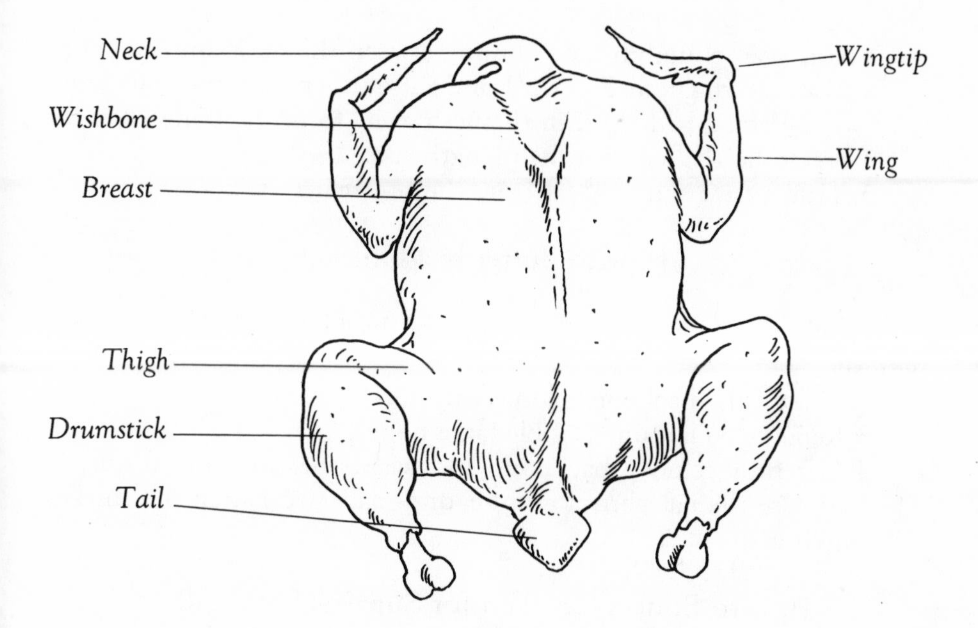

How to Cut a Whole Chicken into Eight Parts

If you want to cut a whole chicken into pieces, follow the next five steps. You will need a chef's knife.

1. Place the chicken on a cutting board, breast side up. Cut off the wingtips and save them for stock. Remove the wings by cutting close to the body of the chicken through the joint that attaches the wing to the breast.

2. With the legs toward you, place the chicken on the back of cutting board. Grasp one leg, slice the skin where the thigh joins the body, lift the chicken, bend the leg back until the thigh joint pops up, then cut around the thigh joint to remove the leg from the body. Repeat with the other leg.

3. Separate the thigh from the drumstick by cutting through the joint, following the yellow line of fat that covers the joint.

4. Make a long incision along one side of the backbone, beginning at the neck and running down to the hind section. Cut along these ribs until the breast meat is removed. Repeat on the other side. You will have one whole breast; split in two as follows:

- Place breast skin side down and make a cut through the V of the wishbone.
- Bend breast back until the keel bone (the large dark bone) pops up.
- Run your thumb or your knife between the meat and keel bone to loosen the flesh. Pull the bone out of the breast (use your knife, if necessary, to help trim the flesh away from the bone). Lay the breast flat and cut it in half lengthwise.

5. Trim excess skin and fat from the breast halves.

How to Butterfly a Chicken

1. Split the chicken's skin along the backbone as described previously.
2. Cut off the backbone along with neck.
3. Remove collarbone (visible large bone).
4. Carefully remove backbone and wishbone, and spread out the chicken. Use the flat part of a knife, or a mallet, to flatten the chicken for cooking.

How to Bone a Chicken for Suprêmes and Fillets

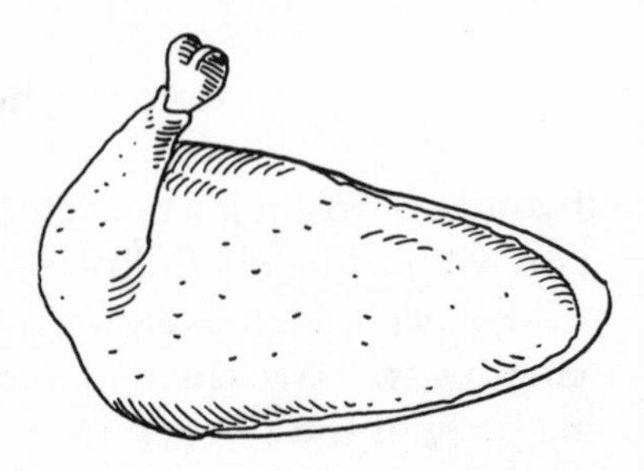

The classic French *suprême* is made by boning the chicken breast and leaving the first joint of the wing attached. To obtain a *fillet*, or "cutlet" as it is sometimes called, the procedure is somewhat different in that the finished product is a boneless, skinless chicken breast that is pounded flat. The supermarket and many cookbooks make no differentiation between a suprême in the French style and a fillet, as the English call it, but for the purposes of this book, I will make the distinction. The easiest solution is to buy a whole chicken and prepare your own suprêmes, storing the remainder of the chicken for another meal.

The only tool you need for either procedure is a boning knife.

For the suprême:

1. Follow directions on previous pages for cutting up a chicken.
2. Beginning at the neck end of the breast, cut along either side of the breast bone by following the outside of the wishbone down to the wing joint.
3. Cut through the wing joint.
4. Sever wings at the second joint (save for stockpot).
5. Cut back from the wing along the ribs to separate the flesh from the bones. Discard the bones.

This will give you two boneless breasts with the first joint of the wing attached. If you don't wish to cut your own suprêmes, and your butcher doesn't know what you are talking about, buy a halved or quartered chicken, which comes with the wings attached, and separate the breasts from the legs, if necessary. Then follow the instructions above to make your suprêmes.

For the fillet or cutlet:

1. Hold the whole breast over a cutting board with skin side down. Bend it backward until the keel bone pops out. Run your thumb between the keel bone and the meat to separate them.
2. Lay the breast on the cutting board, skin side down, and cut the rib cage away from both sides of it.
3. Turn the breast over and cut away the wishbone. Cut the breast in half lengthwise.
4. Remove the skin and the white tendons to prevent the meat from contracting and shrinking during cooking.
5. Place one breast between two sheets of wax paper and pound it thin with a mallet or a rolling pin. Do the same to the other.

How to Bone a Thigh

1. Cut along thin side, joint to joint.
2. Cut meat from one joint. Pull or scrape meat from bone.
3. Cut meat from other joint.

How to Bone a Leg

1. Cut along each side of the thigh bone by slipping your knife under the bone, separating the thigh bone from the meat.
2. Cut all around the joint at the knee to loosen.
3. Scrape down the drumstick bone and pull off.

How to Bone a Whole Chicken

Boning an entire chicken requires a bit of skill and practice. Here are five steps to show you how to do it. If at your first try you end up with torn skin and pieces of the chicken, don't despair. Your skill will improve with time.

STEP 1. Using a sharp boning knife and starting at the neck of the bird, cut along each side of the backbone from neck to tail.

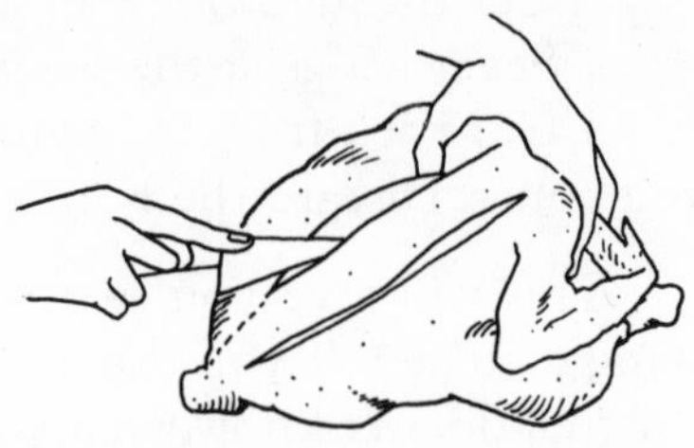

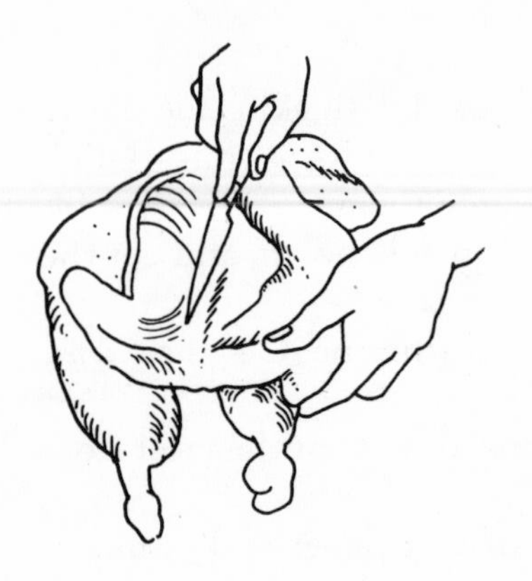

STEP 2. Insert the knife between bone and skin and gently scrape the flesh from the backbone right around to the wishbone at the shoulder joint. Turn chicken and repeat procedure for other side, being careful always to work close to the bone. Cut through the membrane of the wing joint on both sides. Scrape down along the rib cage to expose the collarbone. Continue scraping down the back until you reach the legs (be careful not to pierce the skin, which is very thin at this point). Cut through leg-bone joints.

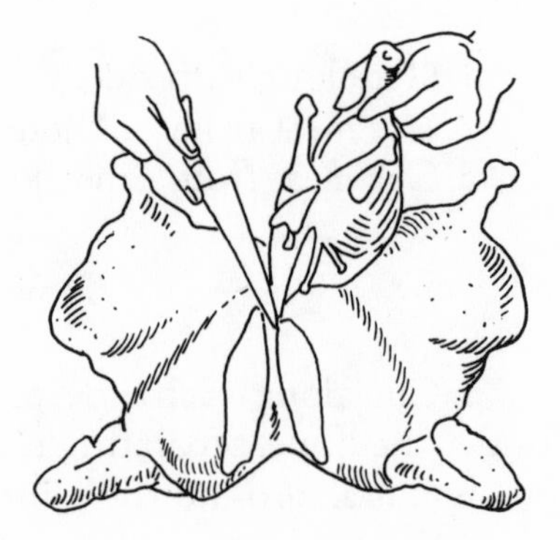

STEP 3. Sever the layer of skin attached to the tailbone. The entire carcass is now free and can be lifted right out. (Save bones for making stock later on.)

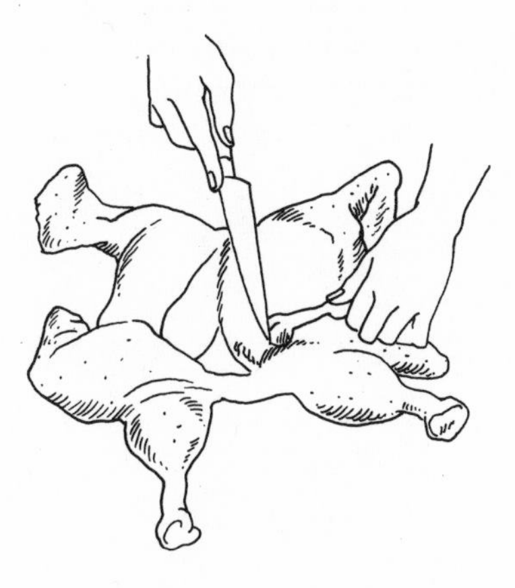

STEP 4. Wiggle and put pressure under the thighbone—the joint will snap right up; cut through the tendons and repeat on the other leg. Debone legs by slicing the meat from the thigh-bone to about one-third of the drum-stick. Cut through the bone (best done with poultry shears) and repeat on the other side.

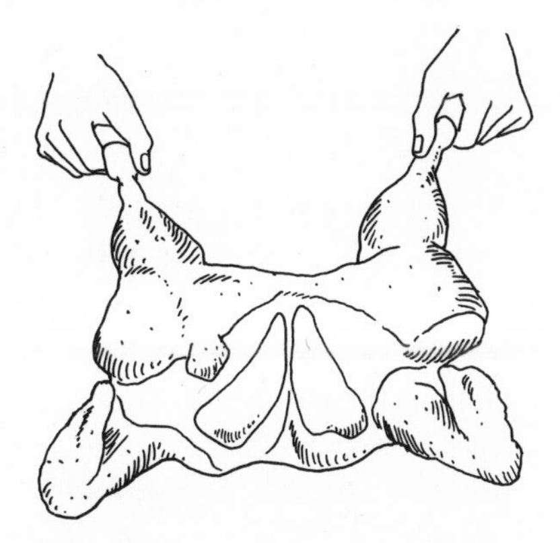

STEP 5. The bird will be as flat as a pancake, with wings and legs still attached. If skin or flesh is cut open in various places, you can sew it up or press it back into place. The bird is now ready for reshaping, using the stuffing of your choice.

How to Carve a Roast Chicken

To carve a roasted chicken, you will need a carving knife and a fork.

1. Remove the chicken from oven and set aside for 10 minutes or so. Place the cooked chicken on a carving board. Holding one drumstick with the fork, cut through the skin between the extended leg and breast section.

2. Gently pull the leg away from the body of the chicken with the fork. Cut down between the thigh bone and the hip to separate the leg completely.

3. Hold the chicken steady by bracing the backbone with the fork. Cut down the breast from top to bottom between the two halves, just to one side of the keel bone.

4. Use the knife in a rocking motion to separate the breast section from the bone. Slice the breast meat for serving. Next, cut through the

shoulder joint where the wing bone is attached to the body. Separate the wing section completely from the carcass. Repeat the entire procedure on the other side of the chicken.

5. Cut the drumsticks apart from the thighs.

Guide to Basic Food Preparations

The following recipes are for food preparations that are included in many of the recipes in this book. Rather than repeat in each recipe, I have decided to place them here for easy reference.

Marinades

Marinades are "spice baths" that help to tenderize the chicken and to add flavor. Here are two methods for making marinades, one uncooked, the other cooked.

1 onion, peeled and cut into quarters
2 shallots, peeled and cut into halves
1 carrot, peeled and cut into chunks
1 celery rib, cut into chunks
1 clove garlic, peeled and chopped
2 cups white or red wine
4 tablespoons vinegar or lemon juice
2 cloves
6 peppercorns
1 bay leaf
1 sprig of fresh thyme, or 1 teaspoon dried thyme
5 tablespoons oil

For the uncooked marinade:

1. Combine all the ingredients.

2. Place the chicken pieces in a dish just large enough to hold them. Pour marinade over the chicken; turn the pieces from time to time, until flavor is absorbed—usually a few hours or overnight.

For the cooked marinade:

1. Heat 2 tablespoons of the oil and sauté the vegetables until they give off some of their liquid. Add the wine, vinegar, spices, and herbs.

2. Simmer the marinade for 30 minutes, then let it cool. Follow preceding instructions for marinating the chicken.

Light Mayonnaise

1 egg yolk
1 tablespoon Dijon-style mustard
2 cups vegetable or olive oil
4 tablespoons tarragon or cider vinegar
4 tablespoons white wine
4 tablespoons low-fat yogurt
White pepper to taste

1. Beat egg yolk and mustard together. Slowly drizzle in the oil, beating with a wire whisk.
2. Add vinegar and wine and fold in yogurt. Season to taste. *Makes 3 cups*

Note: Store mayonnaise in a jar with tight lid; it will keep in the refrigerator for at least 2 weeks.

Pickled Lemons

An essential ingredient in Moroccan cooking, pickled lemons appear in the recipe for Djaj M'Kalli on page 172. These lemons also lend a piquant flavor to many other dishes, particularly salads and vegetable stews.

Lemons (The number of lemons depends on the size of the jar you use.)
Coarse salt, preferably kosher
Freshly squeezed lemon juice

1. Wash lemons. Quarter the lemons from the top to within ½ inch of the bottom, leaving the bottoms attached. Rub inside wedges with salt.
2. Sprinkle salt in the bottom of a glass or stoneware jar with a tight-fitting lid. Squeeze lemons tightly into the jar, pushing them down to release as much juice as possible. If the released juice does not cover the lemons, add as much freshly squeezed lemon juice as necessary.
3. Seal the jar and let the pickled lemons ripen at room temperature. Every so often, shake jar upside down. After 3 weeks the lemons are ready to use; remove the desired amount of lemon, rinse under cold water to remove any traces of salt, and use as directed. Recover the jar.

There is no need for refrigeration, and the lemons last as long as a year, improving with age.

Hint

One or two of these lemons, packed in a decorative jar, make a most welcome gift.

Preserved Fresh Herbs

Fresh herbs will keep their aromatic flavor for about 3 months if preserved in salt. (Do not be put off if the herbs turn dark.)

Fresh herbs *Coarse salt*

1. Remove the leaves of the herbs from the stems; do not wash. Sprinkle the bottom of a small Mason jar with coarse salt. Place one layer of herbs over the salt. Add more salt, repeating this procedure until the jar is full, ending with a layer of salt.
2. Close the jar tightly and keep it in a cool place. When needed, remove the desired amount of herbs, rinse the leaves thoroughly under cold running water, and use.

Bouquet Garni

A combination of herbs tied together in a piece of cheesecloth, a bouquet garni is added to a dish while it is cooking to impart flavor. It is always removed before serving.

The basic bouquet garni consists of:

2 bay leaves
A sprig of parsley
½ teaspoon of dried thyme
2 to 3 whole peppercorns

All-Purpose Chicken Stock

Homemade chicken stock makes a particularly savory sauce or gravy for chicken dishes. It can be frozen in various sizes of containers. It's very helpful to have frozen stock cubes on hand, too. Pour chicken stock into ice-cube trays and chill until set.

1 large stewing hen, trussed (page 6) and blanched (page 8)
Chicken carcasses, bones, or other leftovers (optional)
3 quarts cold water
1 Bouquet Garni (page 17)
4 celery ribs, trimmed
2 leeks, washed and trimmed
1 large onion, unpeeled, studded with cloves
2 carrots, peeled and cut into large chunks
Salt and freshly ground pepper to taste

1. Put the stewing hen and optional leftovers in a large pot. Add the cold water, bring to a boil, and skim. Add the bouquet garni, vegetables, and salt and pepper to taste. Simmer, partly covered, for 2 to 3 hours, occasionally skimming any foam from top. Let stock cool slightly.

2. Strain stock through cheesecloth or a fine sieve to remove all solids. Cool it to room temperature and place, tightly covered, in the refrigerator. When well chilled, skim off all surface fat. *Makes about 2 quarts of stock.*

Note: Although it is always preferable to use homemade chicken stock, you can use canned chicken broth if necessary. Before using, skim off the fat floating on top and, since canned broth contains quite a bit of salt, adjust your seasoning accordingly.

Brown Chicken Stock

1 tablespoon oil
Chicken bones, carcass, wings, and scraps, cut into small pieces
2 onions, sliced
2 carrots, sliced
1 Bouquet Garni (page 17)
2 cups All-Purpose Chicken Stock (page 17)

1. Preheat oven to 425°F. Brush large roasting pan with oil, add chicken pieces, and roast in the oven for 1 hour, turning pieces occasionally.
2. Add vegetables and let them brown for 1 hour more. Remove bones and place them in a large stockpot. Add the bouquet garni, and cover with stock.
3. Simmer, partially covered, for 2 hours, skimming off any scum that rises to the surface. Let cool, taste for seasoning and strength. If a stronger stock is desired, continue cooking, uncovered, to reduce.
4. Strain through a fine sieve to remove solids, and let cool completely. Refrigerate. When stock is cold, remove all the fat and store a small amount in the refrigerator. Freeze the rest, in small batches, for future use.

Brown Deglazing Sauce with Wine

1 tablespoon minced shallot
¼ cup Madeira
⅔ cup brown stock
2 tablespoons finely chopped parsley

1. After sautéing the chicken pieces, stir the minced shallots into the skillet and sauté briefly. Pour in the Madeira and stock, and boil down rapidly over high heat until liquid is syrupy.
2. Pour over the chicken, sprinkle with parsley, and serve.

Fromage Blanc

Fromage blanc is a low-fat, soft white cheese from France that can also be used as a thickening agent in sauces. It is now produced in this country and sold in specialty food stores. If you can't obtain it, here is a recipe that approximates its taste and texture.

1½ cups low-fat ricotta cheese
4 tablespoons low-fat plain yogurt

1. Blend the above ingredients.
2. Store in covered container in the refrigerator for 12 hours before using. Fromage blanc will keep in the refrigerator for 1 week.

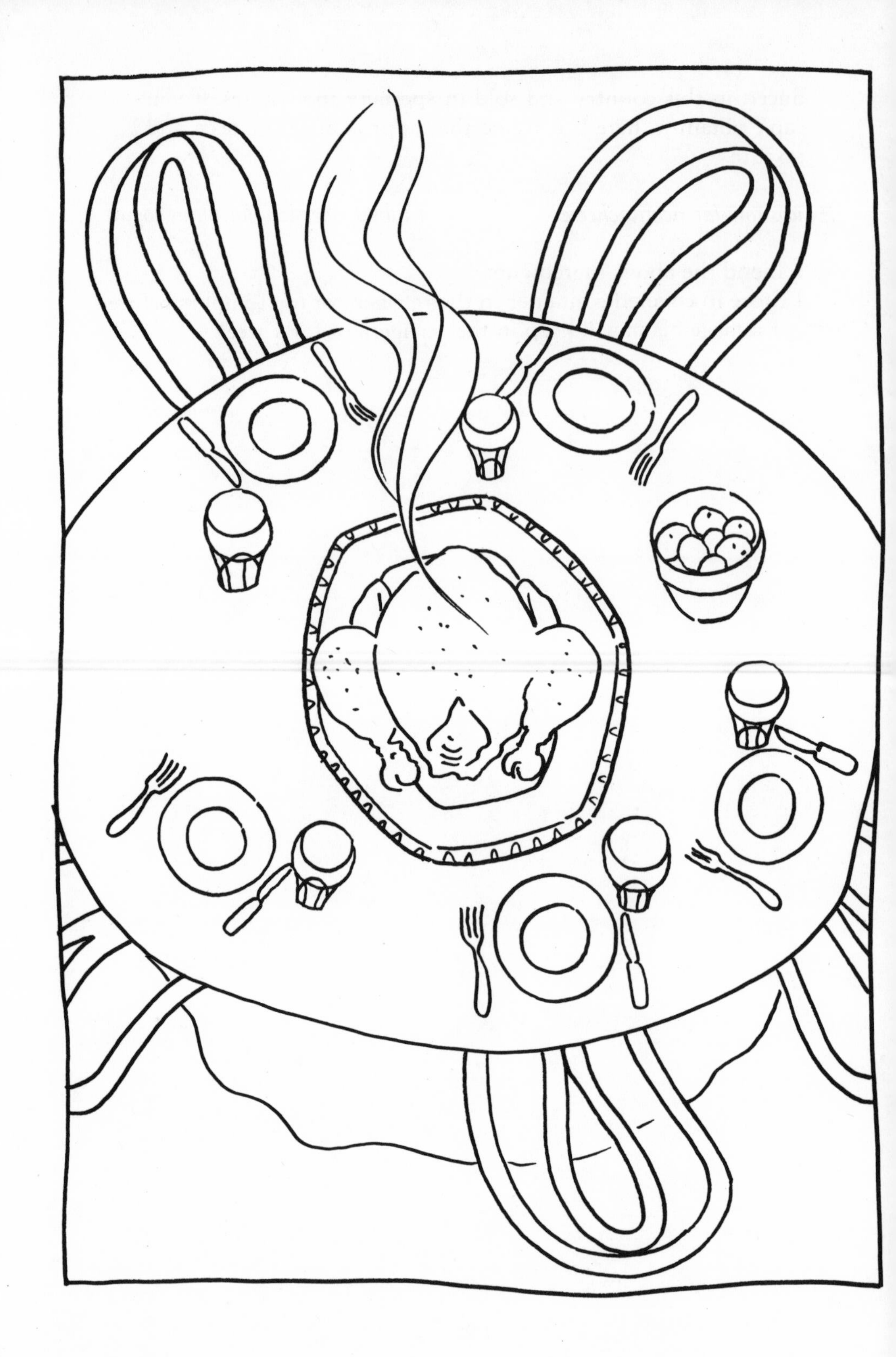

1 Family Dinners

NURTURING begins with nourishment. Gathering around the dining-room table for the evening meal is usually one of the joys of family life. Most of the time it works, but at other times the daily gathering is not that rosy: Children are restless, fathers tense, mothers exhausted. It helps to have a family dinner repertoire that is simple and easy to prepare, but with enough variety to keep the "immovable feast" moving right along.

Basic Roast Chicken

It seems to me that making a classic roast chicken is like wearing basic black. Roast chicken goes with everything, can be dressed up or down, and by making a few changes can move from demure to spectacular. A perfectly cooked roast chicken is chicken at its best, especially when served with boiled red-skinned potatoes and a mixed green salad.

PREPARATION TIME *15 minutes*
COOKING *1 hour and 20 minutes*

One 3½-pound chicken
Pinch of white pepper
Juice of ½ lemon
2 carrots, peeled and sliced into 1-inch chunks
2 small onions, peeled and coarsely chopped
½ cup dry white wine
½ cup chicken stock

1. Preheat oven to 425°F. Pat outside of chicken dry with paper towel. Sprinkle the inside of the chicken with pepper and lemon juice. Truss the chicken as directed on page 6. Place it, breast up, on a rack in a shallow roasting pan in the middle of the preheated oven.
2. Roast chicken for 20 minutes. Reduce heat to 350°F. Place vegetables around chicken.
3. Baste chicken every 15 minutes with rendered juices and a little chicken stock.
4. Roast for approximately 1 hour and 20 minutes, until the drumstick moves easily up and down, or until the juices run clear when the thickest part of the drumstick is pierced with a fork.
5. Remove the chicken from pan, discard trussing string. Let chicken rest at room temperature for at least 10 minutes before carving.
6. Meanwhile, make sauce. Place the roasting pan on a burner. Remove the rack and skim off the fat. Add wine and stock to pan juices and vegetables, and raise heat so the liquid reaches a rapid boil. Scrape up coagulated juices with a wooden spoon, and stir. Adjust seasoning. Pour sauce into a sauceboat and serve separately. *Serves 4.*

Hint

If necessary, chicken can wait 30 minutes in a turned-off, warm oven, with oven door slightly ajar.

Basic Suprêmes with Pan Juices

Theodora FitzGibbon, in *The Food of the Western World,* lists 46 ways of preparing suprêmes, many of which are named after composers, statesmen, royalty, singers, and even a chef.

Sautéed zucchini adds a nice crunch to this basic version.

PREPARATION TIME *5 minutes*
COOKING *10 to 12 minutes*

2 large suprêmes, neatly trimmed (page 10)
½ teaspoon flour
2 teaspoons oil
1 teaspoon butter
Salt and pepper to taste
¼ teaspoon dried thyme
Juice of ½ lemon
1 bunch fresh parsley
4 lemon slices for garnish

1. Dry suprêmes with paper towel and dust with the flour.
2. Heat the oil in a skillet. Add chicken breasts and sauté one side for 3 minutes. Add butter, and sauté for another 2 minutes.
3. Drain fat from pan. Turn suprêmes and dry-sauté second side for 5 to 7 minutes. Remove from heat, season with salt and pepper, and keep warm.
4. Add thyme, lemon juice, and half the parsley, finely chopped, to pan drippings, and stir well. Return suprêmes briefly to warm through, then put on a serving plate.
5. Scrape up juices and spoon over chicken. Top each portion with 2 lemon slices and some parsley sprigs, and serve immediately. *Serves 4.*

Chicken Fricassee

When I was growing up in Germany, capers appeared in most white sauces. Disliking their piquant flavor, I tried to pick them out whenever possible and hide them in my napkin. Tastes change. Now I adore capers, which is why I have put them back into fricassee, where I feel they absolutely belong. For better flavor and a more subtle taste, use the smaller imported variety. Fricassee goes very well with boiled rice and onion crisps.

PREPARATION TIME *12 minutes*
COOKING *1 to 1¼ hours*

One 4-pound chicken, cut into 8 serving pieces and lightly floured
2 tablespoons oil
1 tablespoon butter
½ pound mushrooms, cleaned and cut into quarters
½ cup tarragon vinegar
1 cup chicken stock
Juice of 1 lemon
1 teaspoon sugar
½ cup capers, drained and rinsed
2 tablespoons Fromage Blanc (page 18)
Salt and pepper to taste

1. Wash, dry, and lightly flour the chicken pieces. Heat the oil in a heavy casserole or Dutch oven. Add the chicken pieces, skin side down, and sauté for 2 minutes. Add the butter and sauté for another 2 minutes. Turn the pieces and sauté for about 3 minutes.
2. Remove the chicken pieces and set aside. Sauté the mushrooms until lightly browned. Remove the mushrooms and set aside. Add the vinegar to the casserole, heat through, then add the stock.
3. Return the dark-meat chicken pieces to the pan, cover, and cook over low heat for 20 minutes. Add white-meat pieces and cook for an additional 20 to 30 minutes, or until chicken is cooked through.
4. Return the mushrooms to the casserole and cook for 5 minutes. Add the lemon juice, sugar, and capers.
5. Remove from the heat,* stir in the fromage blanc, taste, and adjust seasoning. Serve directly from the casserole. *Serves 4.*

*This dish may be made up to this point, set aside, and finished just before serving. It takes well to reheating.

Broiled Chicken with Mustard Marinade

This tangy chicken dish mates well with baked polenta and a cucumber salad.

PREPARATION TIME *10 minutes*
COOKING *25 minutes*

Marinade

2 tablespoons oil
1 teaspoon light (low-salt) soy sauce
¼ teaspoon Tabasco
1 tablespoon Dijon-style mustard
2 teaspoons dried rosemary
1 tablespoon mustard seeds
¼ teaspoon ground turmeric

One 3½-pound chicken, quartered
1 small bunch of watercress, stems removed and coarsely chopped

1. Preheat the broiler.
2. Make the marinade: Combine the first four ingredients in a small bowl. Warm the rosemary, mustard seeds, and turmeric in a skillet to bring out their flavor, then add to the marinade. Brush both sides of the chicken pieces with the marinade.
3. Arrange the chicken, skin side down, on a broiling rack. Broil for 10 to 12 minutes, or until nicely browned. Turn the chicken and continue broiling for another 15 minutes.
4. Remove the chicken from the broiler and set aside for 5 minutes or so. Skim fat from drippings, spread sauce over chicken, sprinkle with chopped watercress, and serve. *Serves 4.*

Hint

Turn chicken with a pair of tongs, instead of a fork, to keep in juices.

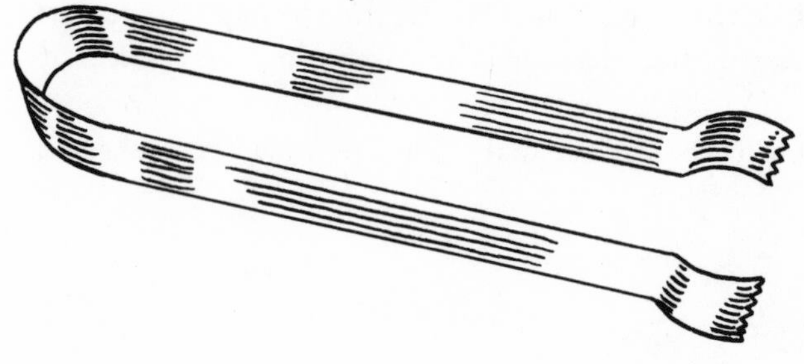

Celeste's Favorite Casserole

Celeste Yazzetti, personnel assistant at Consumers Union, supplied the following convenient family dish. Children like the combination of chicken, pasta, and tomato sauce, and it's easy to prepare and serve.

PREPARATION TIME *10 minutes*
COOKING *1 hour*

One 4-pound chicken, cut into 8 serving pieces
1 clove garlic, minced
1 tablespoon paprika
1 teaspoon dried oregano
1½ cups tomato sauce
One 10-ounce package frozen small peas
½ pound small shell macaroni #23
Chicken stock (optional)
Salt and pepper to taste

1. Preheat oven to 450°F. Trim chicken pieces and place them in a large roasting pan. Brown in the preheated oven for 10 minutes.

2. Reduce heat to 350°F., and add garlic, paprika, oregano, and tomato sauce to the pan with the chicken. Continue to bake chicken for approximately 45 minutes.

3. During last 10 minutes of cooking, add the frozen peas to the pan. Prepare shell macaroni as directed on package, and drain well.

4. Remove the chicken from the pan, and add the cooked shells to the tomato sauce. If more liquid is needed, add additional tomato sauce or chicken stock. Adjust seasoning.

5. Arrange chicken pieces on top of contents in pan. Serve directly from the pan. *Serves 4.*

Lazy Chicken Stew

It's not the chicken that is lazy, it's the cook. Once the dish has been assembled and put into the oven, it practically takes care of itself. It can be made in advance, takes well to reheating, and can be stretched or reduced—an ideal family dish. Serve it with lots of crusty bread for dipping up the sauce.

PREPARATION TIME *20 to 30 minutes*
COOKING *1 hour*

One 4-pound chicken, cut into 12 pieces
1 pound small white onions, peeled
1 pound new potatoes, peeled, left whole if small, otherwise cut into large chunks
½ pound carrots, peeled and cut into 1-inch chunks
4 cloves garlic, peeled and minced
Salt and freshly ground black pepper to taste
1 teaspoon dried thyme, or 4 sprigs fresh
¾ cup white wine
½ cup chicken stock
Chopped parsley

1. Preheat the oven to 450°F.

2. Put the chicken pieces and vegetables in a large oven-proof casserole. Add the garlic, pepper, and thyme, and bake for about 10 minutes.

3. Turn the chicken pieces to allow other sides to brown for an additional 10 minutes or so.

4. Add the wine and stock. Reduce the heat to 350°F., and continue baking, uncovered, for about 40 minutes.

5. Remove the chicken and set aside. Skim the fat off the juices, adjust seasoning, and return chicken to casserole dish. Sprinkle generously with parsley and serve. *Serves 4.*

Mediterranean Chicken

Sauté some garlic and onions, add tomatoes, thyme, and olives. Close your eyes, and you're in Italy. It's worth making this dish for the wonderful aroma alone! Serve it with fresh pasta tossed with basil.

PREPARATION TIME *30 minutes*
COOKING *1 hour*

One 4-pound chicken, cut into quarters
2 tablespoons dried thyme
2 tablespoons olive oil
2 large onions, peeled and cut into slices
4 ripe tomatoes, peeled, seeded, and quartered, or 14 ounces canned tomatoes, partially drained
2 cloves garlic, peeled and crushed
1 cup chicken stock
½ cup Greek black olives, cut into halves and pitted
Salt and freshly ground black pepper to taste

1. Wash the chicken pieces and pat them dry with paper towels. Sprinkle them with thyme.
2. Heat the oil in a large skillet, add chicken parts, and brown on all sides for approximately 25 minutes. Remove and set aside.
3. Sauté onions in same pan until slightly brown and wilted. Remove the onions and skim off the excess fat. Add tomatoes, cooked onions, and crushed garlic, and stir.
4. Return chicken parts to skillet, add stock, cover, and cook over medium heat for 45 minutes, or until tender.
5. Add olives, adjust seasoning, and serve. *Serves 4.*

Chicken Noodle Soup

If it's chicken noodle soup it must be Saturday. At least that's how it was at our house, come rain or shine, summer or winter. Everything was predictable: the golden colored soup, the pale chicken, the overcooked vegetables. The noodles provided suspense. They could be thin one week and thick the next. They might come in the shape of stars, seashells, bows, or, best of all, tiny letters of the alphabet. I'd burn my mouth on the scalding broth, searching for the letters to spell my name, trading with my sisters for a missing *e* or an *l*. Father frowned on this. "You do not play with food." How right he was. Wish he could see me now.

PREPARATION TIME *35 minutes*
COOKING *2½ hours*

One 5- to 6-pound hen or one large chicken*
Coarse salt
Cold water
1 onion, peeled
1 leek, washed and trimmed
1 parsnip, peeled
1 celery root, peeled
Bouquet garni consisting of: 5 sprigs parsley, 2 bay leaves, and 10 peppercorns tied in cheesecloth
2 turnips, peeled and julienned
2 carrots, peeled and julienned
White pepper and salt to taste
½ pound dried egg noodles
Fresh dill, finely chopped

1. Wash and dry chicken thoroughly inside and out. Salt generously, and put in a 6- to 8-quart pot with cold water barely to cover.

2. Add onion, leek, parsnip, celery root, and bouquet garni, and bring to a boil. Reduce heat, simmer uncovered, skimming off foam as it forms. When soup becomes clear after about 45 minutes, reduce heat, cover, and let simmer for 1 hour.

3. Remove vegetables and bouquet garni, and add julienned vegetables. Continue to simmer for another 30 minutes, or until chicken is so tender that the meat begins to fall off the bone.

4. Remove vegetables with a slotted spoon, set aside. Remove chicken, let cool slightly, then remove skin and cut it into quarters, or remove meat entirely from the bones.

5. Strain soup through a very fine sieve and pour ¾ cup of soup over chicken and vegetables to keep them moist. Rinse the original soup pot

and return the remaining soup to it, bring to a bare boil, and add pepper and salt to taste. Cook noodles in soup until tender, following instructions on package.

6. Divide the noodles among 4 hot soup plates, ladle soup over them, sprinkle with dill, and serve piping hot. Serve the chicken and vegetables afterward or combine them in the same dish, if desired. *Serves 4.*

**Note:* Stewing hens are not always available, although many butchers can get one for you. So, although a hen is preferable in a soup because of its flavor and texture, a 4- or 5-pound chicken can be used in its place.

Roasted Chicken with Forty Cloves of Garlic

This is an outrageous-sounding dish. Actually, the cooked garlic cloves are sweet and nutty. The secret is to roast them, unpeeled. Scoop up the sauce, garlic and all, with pieces of crusty peasant bread, and eat. Delicious served with stewed tomatoes.

PREPARATION TIME: *8 minutes*
COOKING: *1 hour and 20 minutes*

One 4-pound chicken, quartered
Crushed black pepper
½ cup oil
40 cloves garlic, unpeeled
Dried sage
Bouquet Garni (page 17)
¼ cup chicken stock

1. Preheat oven to 350°F.

2. Season the chicken quarters with pepper. Heat oil in a large oven-proof and stove-top casserole, or a small Dutch oven.

3. Add garlic and sauté for 3 to 4 minutes until golden brown. Remove the garlic and set it aside. Raise the heat, add the chicken quarters, skin side down, and brown for 4 minutes on each side.

4. Return the garlic cloves to the pan, sprinkle on 1 teaspoon sage, and add bouquet garni. Warm through and pour on the stock, cover, and put the casserole in the preheated oven. Bake for 1 hour, or until chicken is tender.

5. Place chicken on a large serving platter, surround with garlic, sprinkle additional sage over the chicken pieces. Remove the bouquet garni from the casserole, skim fat from juices, adjust seasonings, pour sauce over dish, and serve. *Serves 4.*

Hint

The intensity of garlic can range from pungent to sweet. The finer it is processed, the stronger the flavor. Munching a sprig of fresh parsley after eating garlic, it is said, will cleanse the palate and one's breath.

Chicken Baked in Potato Crust

This is an unusual dish of strong character and crunchy bite—chicken showing its macho side. Serve it with homemade apple-sauce and braised sweet-and-sour red cabbage.

PREPARATION TIME *20 minutes*
COOKING *35 minutes*

One 2½- to 3-pound chicken, cut in half, with backbone and skin removed
1 teaspoon oil
1 tablespoon whole mustard seeds
2 medium baking potatoes (preferably Idaho), peeled
1 egg, slightly beaten
1 medium yellow onion, peeled and grated
1 tablespoon prepared Pommery mustard

1. Preheat oven to 425°F.
2. Rub chicken lightly with oil. Place the chicken, skin side down, in an ovenproof dish. Sprinkle with mustard seeds. Put into the pre-heated oven and roast for 10 minutes.
3. Meanwhile grate the potatoes on the large holes of a grater. Place the potatoes in a piece of cheesecloth, and wring out excess moisture. Add the egg and grated onion to the potatoes, and mix well.
4. Remove the chicken from the oven, spread Pommery mustard over the skin side, and cover with a thin, even layer of the potato mixture.
5. Return the chicken to the oven, and bake for 20 to 25 minutes. If a browner crust is desired, place the chicken under a preheated broiler for a few minutes. *Serves 4.*

Hint

Grate the potatoes shortly before using them since they turn brown quickly. Although this does not affect the flavor, it does mar the appearance of the dish.

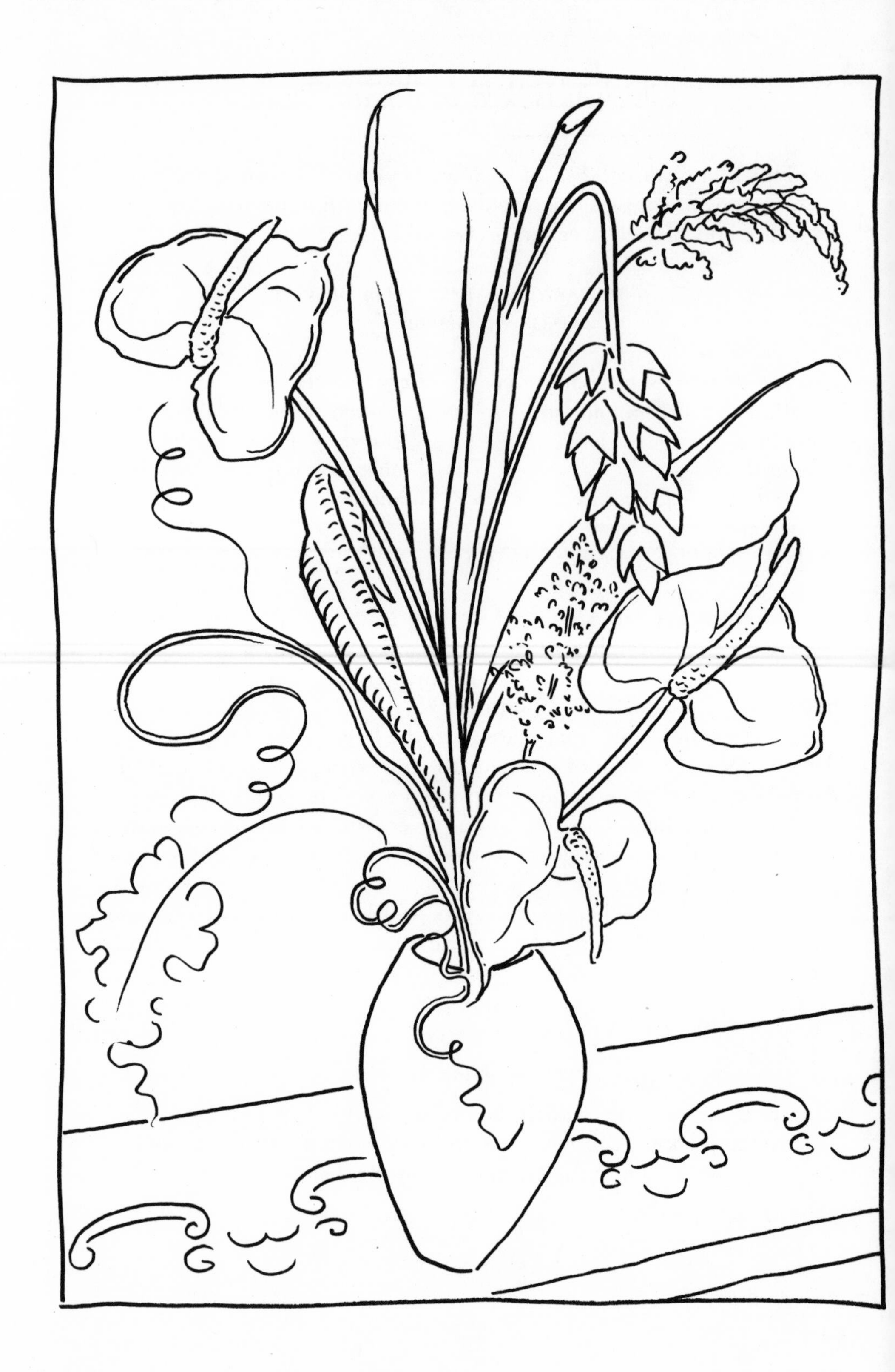

2

Formal Dinners

ANTHELME Brillat-Savarin, the nineteenth-century French dictator of gastronomical etiquette, gave the sophisticated diners of his day his suggestions for a successful dinner party, all of which are still sound today. None is more appropriate than: "Let the dishes be few in number, but exquisitely choice."

His British counterpart Dr. William Kitchener, author of *The Affairs of the Mouth,* went one step further. He frequently issued the following dinner invitations: "The honour of your company is requested.... The first specimen will be on the table at five o'clock precisely, when the business of the day will immediately commence." He locked the door at five, his motto being "better never than late."

Baked Chicken with Crayfish or Shrimp

Crayfish, also called *crawfish* or *crawdaddy*, is a small freshwater cousin of the lobster. Sweet and succulent and considered a great delicacy, the meat takes considerable skill to extract, which, to crayfish aficionados, is all part of the fun. Serve the dish with boiled white rice and steamed asparagus tips.

PREPARATION TIME *20 minutes*
COOKING *50 minutes*

One 3½-pound chicken, cut into 16 serving pieces
Crushed black pepper
4 tablespoons oil
12 crayfish, or large shrimp, shelled and deveined
8 shallots, finely chopped
2 cloves garlic, sliced
4 tablespoons cognac
2 tomatoes, diced
1 tablespoon dried tarragon
1 cup white wine
1 cup chicken stock
10 large, fresh shiitake mushrooms, cut into quarters
Chopped parsley for garnish

1. Preheat oven to 400°F.

2. Season the chicken pieces with pepper. Heat a large ovenproof, stove-top casserole or frying pan, add oil, and sauté the crayfish or shrimp until they turn red, about 1 minute. Remove and set aside.

3. Brown the chicken pieces, skin side down, 4 or 5 minutes on each side. Add the shallots and garlic, and stir. Raise heat. Add the cognac and flambé (page 5).

4. Add the tomatoes and tarragon, and stir to combine. Add the wine and stock, and heat through. Add the mushrooms, and bring to a boil.

5. Put casserole into the preheated oven and bake, covered, for 35 to 40 minutes. Remove from the oven and transfer the contents of the casserole to a warm serving platter. If necessary, reduce the liquid remaining in the casserole and pour it over the chicken. Decorate the platter with the shellfish and garnish with chopped parsley. *Serves 4.*

Squabs with Shallot Crisps

I have included squab in this cookbook because although it is not really a chicken, it is more or less in the same family. Its dark and slightly gamey meat is a great delicacy and it is an essential feature of several outstanding recipes. This particular dish is delicious when served with wild rice and leeks braised in a little butter and oil.

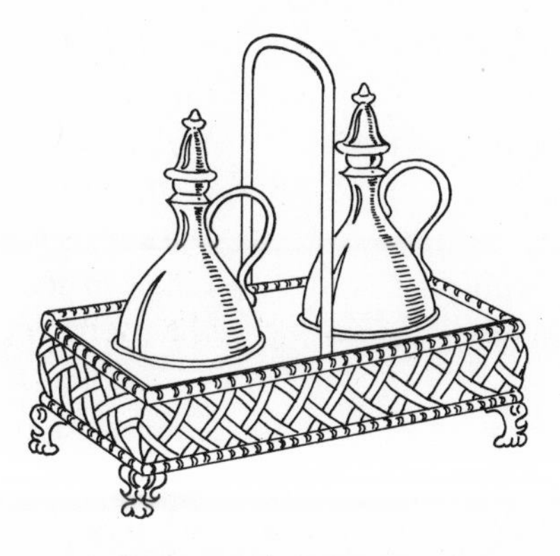

PREPARATION TIME *10 minutes*
COOKING *25 minutes*

4 squabs, cut into halves, with wings removed
Salt and pepper to taste
4 tablespoons olive oil
12 shallots, julienned
¼ cup cognac
½ cup chicken stock
2 tablespoons butter
Black truffle pieces (optional)

1. Preheat oven to 375°F.
2. Season squabs with salt and pepper. Heat a large skillet, add the olive oil, and sauté the squabs, skin side down, on both sides for 5 to 7 minutes per side.
3. Add the shallots, sauté for another 5 minutes, until crisp and firm. Remove shallots and squabs and set aside. Drain off the fat.
4. Raise heat, pour cognac in the skillet, and flambé (page 5). When flame has subsided, add the stock and swirl in the butter. Add the optional truffles and taste for seasoning.
5. Place squabs in a baking dish, pour the sauce over them, and sprinkle tops with shallots. Bake in the preheated oven for about 10 minutes. *Serves 4.*

White Wine Chicken Stew

This entire dish can be made ahead of time and kept frozen in a plastic pouch. It is delectable served with a purée of leeks and potatoes.

PREPARATION TIME *15 minutes*
COOKING *45 minutes*

One 3½-pound chicken, cut into 8 pieces
3 tablespoons oil
4 shallots, finely chopped
1 tablespoon cognac
1 cup white wine, preferably Riesling
2 bay leaves
Pinch of nutmeg
Pinch of tarragon
Pinch of black pepper
½ pound mushrooms, cleaned and cut into quarters
Juice of ½ lemon
Chicken stock if needed
½ teaspoon cornstarch, dissolved in water, to form a paste
Chopped parsley for garnish

1. Wash the chicken pieces and dry with paper towels. Heat 2 tablespoons oil in a large skillet. Add the chicken pieces and sauté over medium-high heat on both sides until brown. Lower heat, add the shallots, and cook for 2 minutes.

2. Pour on the cognac and ignite. When the flames have died, add the wine, bay leaves, nutmeg, tarragon, and pepper. Bring to a quick boil, then reduce heat and simmer for 25 to 35 minutes.

3. Meanwhile, heat the remaining oil in a separate pan and sauté the mushrooms until they brown. Add the lemon juice, then combine the mushrooms with the chicken. Remove the bay leaves and transfer the chicken pieces to a serving dish.

4. If more liquid is needed in the sauce, add more wine or some stock. Add the dissolved cornstarch to the sauce, and mix well until sauce thickens. Adjust seasoning.* Spoon the sauce over the chicken, sprinkle with chopped parsley, and serve. *Serves 4.*

*If the dish is to be stored, let it cool at this point, then put it, together with the sauce, into a plastic bag and freeze.

Sautéed Suprêmes with Honey-Mustard Glaze, Peppers, and Zucchini

This is an easy and tasty way to prepare suprêmes. Fried parsley (see Hint below) and baked eggplant Provençale make perfect accompaniments.

PREPARATION TIME *30 minutes*
COOKING *35 minutes*

3 tablespoons oil
2 red peppers, cored and cut into strips
2 yellow peppers, cored and cut into strips
2 small zucchini, cut into thin strips
Salt, thyme, and pepper to taste
1 tablespoon butter
8 chicken suprêmes (page 10)
2 tablespoons honey
4 tablespoons Dijon-style mustard
Juice of 1 lime

1. Preheat the broiler.

2. Pour 2 tablespoons oil into skillet, and sauté the peppers for 10 minutes; remove and reserve. Sauté zucchini for about 10 minutes, season to taste with salt, thyme, and pepper. Remove zucchini and set aside.

3. Heat the remaining tablespoon of oil and the butter in the skillet. Sauté the chicken breasts for about 6 minutes on each side; remove and reserve. Pour off the fat and wipe the skillet.

4. Return the skillet to the burner, and add the honey. As it begins to foam, add the mustard. Stir vigorously, then add the lime juice. Cook through and adjust seasonings. Slash the chicken on the diagonal (about ¼ inch deep). Spread the honey-mustard sauce over chicken pieces.

4. Combine the vegetables and arrange them on a flameproof platter, then top with the chicken and sauce to form an attractive color scheme. Place under preheated broiler for 3 minutes. Serve immediately. *Serves 4.*

Hint

Although parsley is usually treated as a garnish or a salad ingredient, it also makes a delicious side dish: Take 1 bunch of parsley, cut the stems to 1 inch in length, and wash and dry them *thoroughly*. Heat 1 teaspoon each butter and oil in a skillet until foaming. Add the parsley and toss until crisp and crunchy to the taste.

Baked Chicken with Fennel Sauté

"The fennel is beyond every other vegetable, delicious. It greatly resembles in appearance the largest size celery, perfectly white, and there is no vegetable equals it in flavor. It is eaten at dessert crude and with, or without dry salt, indeed I preferred it to every other vegetable, or to any fruit."

—THOMAS JEFFERSON, *Garden Book*

Accompanying servings of scalloped parsley potatoes and roasted red peppers lend color to this tasty dish.

PREPARATION TIME *20 minutes*
COOKING *1 hour and 20 minutes*

4 small fennel bulbs, quartered
2 tablespoons oil
2 medium onions, chopped
2 cloves garlic, whole, unpeeled
1 cup chicken stock
Pinch salt and freshly ground black pepper to taste
1 teaspoon fennel seeds
1 tablespoon chopped fresh basil, or 1 teaspoon dry
2 bay leaves
Two 2½-pound chickens, quartered
2 teaspoons tomato paste
¼ cup white wine
Dash of Pernod
Chicken stock (optional)
Chopped parsley for garnish
Chopped fennel tops for garnish

1. Preheat the oven to 400°F.

2. Parboil fennel pieces in boiling water for 3 minutes, drain, set aside.

3. Heat 1 tablespoon oil in a large skillet, sauté the onions and garlic until they turn translucent, over medium heat about 5 minutes. Add the fennel, sauté for 5 minutes, then add the chicken stock, reduce heat, cover, and let simmer for 10 minutes, or until the fennel is tender yet still crunchy. Transfer the vegetables to a large ovenproof casserole, sprinkle with salt, pepper, fennel seeds, basil, and bay leaves, and set aside.

4. Dry the chicken pieces with paper towels. Using the same skillet, raise heat, add the remaining oil, sauté the chicken, skin side down first, for about 6 minutes on each side, or until brown. Arrange the chicken over the vegetable mixture.

5. Deglaze pan drippings with tomato paste, wine, and Pernod, and pour over the chicken. Cover the casserole and place in the preheated oven. After 15 minutes, reduce heat to 350°F., adding some chicken stock if necessary. Bake for 30 additional minutes, or until chicken is tender.

6. When ready to serve, remove the skin if desired, arrange chicken on a warm platter, surround with fennel pieces. Discard the bay leaves, skim off excess fat, add additional Pernod if desired, and adjust seasoning. Pour the sauce over the dish and garnish with chopped parsley and fennel greens. *Serves 4.*

Roasted Capon Breast with Stewed Fruit

Baked kasha and purée of summer squash complement this rich dish.

PREPARATION TIME *25 minutes*
COOKING *1 hour*

1 large capon breast (about 3 to 4 pounds)
White pepper
Grated zest of ½ orange
2 tablespoons oil
½ pound Italian plums, in season, or pitted prunes
2 apples
1 pear
1 tablespoon butter
Juice of ½ lemon
¼ cup dry white wine
2 ounces shelled walnuts for garnish
Fresh mint leaves for garnish

1. Preheat oven to 350°F.
2. Pat capon breast dry with paper towels. Pepper both sides and sprinkle with orange zest.
3. Heat the oil in a combination stove-top and ovenproof pan. Sauté the capon over high heat, about 5 minutes on each side, until browned. Place in the preheated oven and roast for 35 to 40 minutes, turning once.
4. Meanwhile remove the pits from the plums and cut them into quarters. Cut the apples and pear in half lengthwise (do not peel), core them, and cut into wedges.
5. Melt the butter in a skillet, add the lemon juice and wine, then add the fruit. Cover, and let simmer for 8 minutes. Remove the fruit with a slotted spoon and keep it warm until serving time.
6. Carve the breast into thick slices, place on a serving platter, and surround with stewed fruits. Garnish with walnuts and mint leaves. *Serves 4.*

Chicken Baked in Bread

This dish is so stunning it never, never fails to solicit ohs and ahs when presented. Actually it is easy to make, particularly when you use frozen dough. The flavors are enhanced by accompanying the dish with a colorful ratatouille.

RISING TIME *2 hours*
PREPARATION TIME *20 minutes*
COOKING *1½ hours*

1 package frozen pizza dough
One 3½-pound chicken
2 teaspoons butter
1 tablespoon oil
½ pound mushrooms, preferably fresh porcini
3 shallots, peeled and chopped
1 chicken liver
½ teaspoon dried rosemary
Salt and pepper to taste
1 teaspoon cognac

1. Let the pizza dough rise as instructed on the package.

2. As the raw chicken will be standing for 1 hour, make sure you wash inside and outside of chicken thoroughly; pat dry the exterior and inside cavity.

3. Heat the butter and 1 teaspoon oil in a large skillet. Sauté mushrooms and shallots until slightly brown, about 5 minutes. Add the chicken liver, rosemary, and salt and pepper to taste. Sauté for 2 minutes. Add the cognac, heat through, adjust seasoning, let cool slightly.

4. Stuff this mixture into the chicken cavity. Tie legs together with twine.

5. Pull or roll pizza dough into a large square, about ½ inch thick. Place chicken in center. Fold dough over chicken, sealing perfectly. Rub the surface of the dough with 1 teaspoon oil, place chicken in dough on a baking sheet, cover with a clean towel, and let stand in a warm spot for no longer than 1 hour.

6. Preheat the oven to 400°F.

7. Bake for 30 minutes, uncovered, or until the top has formed a nice brown crust. Reduce oven temperature to 350°F., cover top loosely with foil, and continue baking for 1 hour. Remove foil. Brush the top with remaining teaspoon oil and bake, uncovered, for 5 minutes. Remove chicken from the oven and let it rest for 15 minutes. Transfer to a serving dish and bring directly to the table to serve. *Serves 4.*

Ballotine with Risotto, Sun-Dried Tomatoes, and Olives

This dish takes some time to prepare, but the results are well worth the time and effort. Artichokes in parsley sauce is a good accompaniment to this elegant dish.

PREPARATION TIME *50 minutes*
COOKING *1 hour and 20 minutes*

6 sun-dried tomatoes soaked in 1 tablespoon extra-virgin olive oil
Olive oil
2 green onions, chopped
2 cups chicken stock, more if needed
1 cup rice, preferably Italian Arborio (short-grained)
12 black olives, pitted and roughly chopped
12 green olives, pitted and roughly chopped
1 egg white, lightly beaten
Salt and black pepper to taste
One 3½-pound whole chicken, boned (page 12)

To prepare sun-dried tomatoes:

1. Soak the sun-dried tomatoes in hot water for 15 minutes. Drain them well, and cover with oil. When ready to use, remove them from the oil and prepare as directed. Prepared sun-dried tomatoes may be stored in a tightly covered jar in the refrigerator for up to 2 weeks.

To prepare risotto:

2. Heat 1 teaspoon olive oil in a skillet, add the green onions, and sauté until translucent, about 4 minutes.
3. In a separate pan, bring 2 cups chicken stock to the boiling point. Add the rice to the skillet with the onions, and sauté to coat, stirring constantly.
4. Start adding hot stock, about ½ cup at a time, and stir. Keep adding stock once the previously added liquid is completely absorbed. The risotto should be *al dente* in 20 minutes.

To make the ballotine:

5. Preheat oven to 350°F.
6. Drain and add sun-dried tomatoes, the black and green olives, and salt and pepper to taste to the cooked risotto. Fold in the egg white, adjust seasoning, and let the mixture cool slightly.

7. Stuff the cavity of the boned chicken with the risotto mixture. Fold over one end of stuffed chicken, then the other. Secure the stuffed chicken with twine tied in butcher or post-office knots, about 1½ inches apart, and secure any additional openings with toothpicks.

8. Lightly coat the bottom of an ovenproof casserole with olive oil. Place the stuffed chicken in it and put into the preheated oven. After 20 minutes, add a little bit of water (this will help the browning effect). Baste every 10 minutes with pan drippings. Roast chicken for approximately 25 minutes. When ready, remove from the oven, and let cool for 10 minutes before removing toothpicks and twine. Slice and serve. *Serves 4.*

Cornish Hen Demi-deuil, with Apple-and-Onion Stuffing

In French, *demi-deuil* means "half-mourning." As a culinary term, it refers to chicken prepared with black truffles. "Truffles taste like truffles and like nothing else," said Waverly Root. Indeed, the unique flavor and aroma of this mysterious black fungus is hard to describe. Found primarily in the Dordogne area in France, truffles are expensive because they are so scarce. Fortunately a bit of black truffle goes a long way in heightening the flavor of any food with which it comes in contact. The dish goes well with potato gnocchi.

PREPARATION TIME *25 minutes*
COOKING *45 minutes*

4 small Cornish hens
Juice of 1 lemon
White pepper to taste
1 ounce fresh black truffles, finely chopped*
3 cups cored, peeled, and chopped Granny Smith apples
3 cups peeled and chopped Spanish onions
1 tablespoon butter
Salt and pepper to taste
Watercress for garnish

1. Preheat oven to 425°F.
2. Remove lower wingtips of hens and sprinkle insides of each with lemon juice and pepper.
3. Divide truffles into 4 portions. Carefully loosen upper skin of hens and slip truffles under skin of breast.
4. Combine chopped apples and onions. Stuff each hen with this mixture, reserving any leftover stuffing.
5. Truss birds as directed on page 6.
6. Place birds in a roasting pan and put into the preheated oven, breast side up. Roast for 20 to 25 minutes on each side, or until done. Remove and discard the trussing twine and let the birds sit for 5 minutes.
7. Cut each bird in half, remove backbone and stuffing.

8. Heat butter in a skillet, add pan drippings and all the stuffing, and sauté over high heat for 5 minutes. Season lightly with salt and pepper.

9. Arrange hens on a large serving platter, skin side up. Garnish with watercress and serve with apple-and-onion mixture. *Serves 4.*

*If fresh truffles are not available, use the canned variety. "First cooking" (or "first boiling") on label indicates that the truffle has been cooked once—making it by far the best-tasting and the most costly. Subsequent boiling, which is done to obtain a strong truffle juice, reduces the flavor of the truffle and, with it, the price.

Hint

To get the most out of fresh truffles, moisten chopped truffle pieces with a bit of olive oil, slip under breast skin, wrap bird loosely, and allow the perfume of the truffles to penetrate for a few hours or overnight.

3

Everyday Lunches

TODAY, everyday lunch usually means a simple meal. Some take it like clockwork at 12:00 noon; others grab something whenever they find a moment. Almost everybody agrees it should be light and readily available.

Napoleon, for one, was an early fast-food fan. The moment he felt hungry, his appetite had to be satisfied. His household was arranged accordingly: The minute the emperor expressed a desire to eat, a roast chicken was forthcoming. Napoleon's chef took no chances; no matter where and when, he roasted a fresh chicken every 20 minutes.

That probably was considered an extravagance, even then. Far better to have lunch ready by either preparing it ahead of time, or by opting for a dish that requires little time to make.

Broiled Roulades with Duxelle

Spinach pilaf and grilled tomato halves sprinkled with thyme would make a satisfying accompaniment to this dish.

PREPARATION TIME *30 minutes*
COOKING *40 minutes*

4 whole boneless, skinless chicken breasts, cut in half, trimmed, and pounded to make very thin fillets
Crushed black peppercorns
2 teaspoons lemon juice
1 pound mushrooms, finely chopped
2 teaspoons butter
2 teaspoons oil
4 shallots, peeled and minced
¼ cup chicken stock
2 teaspoons finely chopped fresh chives
1 tablespoon Madeira (optional)
Salt and pepper to taste
Parsley sprigs for garnish
Oil to coat

1. Season the fillets with pepper and lemon juice, and set aside.

2. To make duxelle filling: A handful at a time, place the chopped mushrooms in a towel and twist tightly into a ball to extract as much juice as possible. Heat the butter and oil in a large skillet, and sauté shallots until translucent. Add mushrooms, and sauté over fairly high heat until brown, about 7 minutes, stirring constantly. Pour in the stock, and continue cooking for another 10 minutes. Add chives and optional Madeira, and adjust seasoning.

3. Preheat the broiler.

4. Spread about 1 tablespoon of duxelle filling evenly over each fillet. Roll up the fillets, starting at pointed edge, and tuck in the ends.*

5. Brush tops of the roulades with oil and place them on middle rack of the broiler. Broil for 8 to 10 minutes on each side, until lightly browned. Remove and let cool slightly. Trim edges and serve either whole, or sliced into 1-inch rounds, over a bed of spinach pilaf. *Serves 4.*

*Can be made in advance up to this point.

Lettuce Boats with Chicken and Pine Nuts

This light dish is perfect for the day when you don't know who wants to eat when. Prepared within minutes and served buffet-style, it has the added attraction of being slightly exotic. For easy cutting, begin with semifrozen chicken breasts. Serve with fried rice.

PREPARATION TIME *15 minutes*
COOKING *6 minutes*

1 whole boneless and skinless chicken breast (about 8 ounces)

Marinade

1 egg
2 tablespoons cornstarch
1 tablespoon light (low-salt) soy sauce

1 head of iceberg lettuce
⅓ cup corn or peanut oil
½ cup finely chopped canned winter bamboo shoots
1 cup finely chopped celery
1 small can water chestnuts, drained
6 dried mushrooms, soaked, with stems removed, and finely chopped
½ cup finely chopped scallions
2 tablespoons dry sherry
1 teaspoon sugar
Salt to taste
½ cup pine nuts

1. Chop chicken into ½-inch chunks and put into a mixing bowl. Add the marinade, mix well, and set aside.

2. Separate the lettuce leaves and trim them into small cups or "boats," about 16 pieces in all. Put them in a plastic bag and keep in the refrigerator.

3. Heat a wok or skillet over moderate heat, add ¼ cup oil, and heat. Add the chicken and stir to separate the pieces. Add remaining oil to skillet. Add bamboo shoots, celery, water chestnuts, mushrooms and scallions, and stir-fry for 2 minutes. Sprinkle with sherry and sugar, and stir once more. Adjust seasonings.

4. Arrange on a serving dish and garnish top with pine nuts. Place lettuce leaves on a separate serving dish and invite each diner to place about 2 tablespoons of the chicken mixture on a lettuce boat, roll it into a "package," and eat. *Serves 4.*

Favorite Chicken Salad

Radicchio, a member of the chicory family with a slightly bitter taste, is of Northern Italian origin. A status item of late, it is priced accordingly. One of radicchio's virtues is its color, which is purplish red. The same effect can be achieved by using red cabbage, whose leaves make a spectacular underlining for my favorite chicken salad. A basket of breadsticks and rolls and a platter of crudités would complete this dish nicely.

PREPARATION TIME *25 minutes*
COOKING *45 minutes*

One 3-pound chicken
Water
1 onion studded with 6 cloves
2 bay leaves

Mayonnaise Dressing

1 egg yolk
Juice of ½ lemon
½ cup oil
2 tablespoons plain low-fat yogurt
1 teaspoon fresh orange juice
1 tablespoon fresh dill, chopped, or 1 teaspoon dried
Pinch curry powder
Salt and freshly ground black pepper to taste

½ cup raisins
2 medium tart apples, peeled, cored, and cut into small cubes
Red cabbage leaves
Watercress for garnish

1. Wash the chicken thoroughly inside and out.

2. Put water, onion, and bay leaves in a large kettle, and bring to a boil. Add the chicken, reduce heat, and let simmer, partially covered, for 35 minutes.

3. While the chicken is cooking, make the mayonnaise. Put egg yolks in a mixing bowl. Add lemon juice, stirring with a wire whisk. Gradually add oil, stirring briskly. Stir in yogurt, orange juice, dill, curry powder, a generous portion of black pepper, and salt to taste. Refrigerate.

4. Remove pot from heat, and let stand, uncovered, for 20 minutes. When the chicken has cooled, remove, and discard skin. Separate all joints (this is best done by hand) and cut meat into large bite-size portions. Place the meat in a large dish, add the raisins and apples.*

5. Fold the mayonnaise into the chicken. Line a serving platter with red cabbage leaves and fill with salad. Surround with watercress. *Serves 4.*

*This dish may be made ahead of time and assembled just before serving. However, it does taste best when assembled shortly after the chicken has been cooked, while it is still slightly warm.

Stir-fried Chicken Cubes with Fresh Ginger

This dish is easy and quick to make and will delight everyone with its combination of subtle flavors. A beansprout-and-tofu salad and sticky rice are authentic accompaniments to this dish.

PREPARATION TIME *12 minutes*
COOKING *5 minutes*

1 to 2 tablespoons oil
1½ pounds boneless and skinless chicken breasts, cut into small cubes
3 scallions, chopped
1 clove garlic, minced
2 small carrots, cut into small cubes
1-inch piece fresh ginger, peeled and grated
2 tablespoons oyster sauce, or light (low-salt) soy sauce*
½ teaspoon sugar
¼ cup white wine
Pepper to taste
2 tablespoons chopped fresh cilantro or Italian parsley

1. Heat oil in a wok or a nonstick frying pan.
2. Add chicken, scallions, garlic, and carrots, and stir-fry until chicken turns white (about 1 minute).
3. Add ginger and sauce; toss until chicken is cooked (about 2 minutes). Remove chicken and vegetable mixture and set aside in a warm dish.
4. Add sugar, wine, and pepper to pan, and boil to reduce. Adjust seasoning.
5. Return chicken to pan, add cilantro or parsley, and toss briefly. Serve at once. *Serves 4.*

*These sauces are available in all Oriental grocery stores and in many supermarkets.

Hint

When buying fresh ginger, choose one with a smooth, firm skin. It will keep for weeks in a plastic bag in the refrigerator.

Poached Chicken in Broth with Watercress and Other Vegetables

This dish, suggested by my health-conscious friend, Mel Wolf, has qualities often found in Japanese cooking: a pleasing blend of colors and texture, an elegant simplicity, and a pure taste. Preparing the dish a day ahead of time makes it easy to remove any excess fat from the broth, and the entire dish can be assembled in a short time.

PREPARATION TIME *20 minutes*
COOKING *1 hour and 40 minutes*

One 3-pound chicken
1 large onion, studded with cloves
Bouquet Garni (page 17)
One 2-inch piece of fresh ginger, peeled
2½ quarts chicken stock
4 carrots, cleaned and cut into 2-inch pieces
2 parsnips, cleaned and cut into 2-inch pieces
8 small potatoes, peeled and cut into halves
2 cups watercress, stems removed
Prepared red horseradish

1. Clean the chicken, put the onion into the cavity, and truss as directed on page 6. Add the bouquet garni and ginger to stock in a 5- or 6-quart stockpot. Bring the liquid to a boil, reduce heat, and add chicken. Cover, and simmer for 45 minutes.

2. Add carrots and parsnips to the stock, and continue to simmer for an additional 15 minutes.

3. Remove the chicken and allow it to cool. Remove the vegetables and store them in the refrigerator. Allow the broth to cool; remove bouquet garni and ginger, and discard. Cool broth and then refrigerate several hours or overnight.

4. When chicken is cool enough to handle, remove twine, onion, and skin, and discard. Remove chicken from bones and cut it into serving-size pieces. Cover and store in refrigerator.*

5. About 1 hour before serving, remove the broth, vegetables, and

*This dish can be made in advance to this point.

chicken from the refrigerator. Remove any fat from the top of the broth. Bring the broth to a boil, reduce heat, add potatoes, and simmer for 30 minutes.

6. Add the chicken to the pot and allow it to heat through, about 2 minutes. Remove potatoes and chicken to a heated platter. Keep warm. Add carrots and parsnips to broth; simmer while you assemble the rest of the dish.

7. Place ½ cup of watercress leaves in each of 4 soup bowls; add equal amounts of broth, carrots, and parsnips to each bowl. Serve chicken and potatoes with generous amounts of horseradish, along with broth and vegetables. *Serves 4.*

Chicken and Scallops Steamed over Dill and Seaweed

What is a barnyard fowl doing on a bed of seaweed, next to shellfish? Striking up an exciting culinary match, that's what. Similar in texture and appearance, the delicate flavors of chicken and scallops complement each other beautifully. Tomato rice is a colorful and tasty addition to this dish.

PREPARATION TIME *10 minutes*
COOKING *10 minutes*

1 bunch fresh dill, with stems
*1 package frozen seaweed**
1 fennel bulb, quartered
One 10-ounce package frozen lima beans or Italian beans, cooked as directed
2 whole boneless and skinless chicken breasts, cut into pieces the same size as scallops
1 pound bay scallops or sea scallops, quartered or halved
2 teaspoons sweet paprika
Juice of ½ lemon
Salt and pepper to taste
Lemon wedges for garnish

1. Line a steamer basket with fresh dill sprigs and seaweed. Arrange fennel and beans over it in an attractive pattern. Do the same with the chicken and scallops.

2. Heat water in a large kettle to a rapid boil. Place steamer basket over it, cover, and steam for 10 to 11 minutes.

3. Remove basket from kettle. Sprinkle paprika over the scallops and chicken, and lemon juice over the vegetables. Season with salt and pepper to taste and decorate with lemon wedges, cover. Set basket on a plate and bring it directly to the table to serve. *Serves 4.*

*Frozen seaweed is commonly sold at Korean and Japanese markets. If it isn't available, substitute fresh spinach leaves.

Chicken Strips Sautéed with Garlic, Olives, and Spices

This savory dish can be prepared quickly, particularly if all the chopping and slicing has been done beforehand. I like to serve it with a celery and mushroom salad.

PREPARATION TIME *12 minutes*
COOKING *12 minutes*

1 tablespoon oil
3 cloves garlic, crushed
1 medium yellow onion, chopped
1 bunch scallions, chopped, including green tops
8 green Greek olives, rinsed, pitted, and chopped
1½ teaspoons ground cumin
1½ teaspoons ground coriander
Dash of cayenne
4 whole boneless and skinless chicken breasts, cut into ½-inch strips
1 tablespoon dry vermouth
½ to ¾ cups chicken stock
2 teaspoons sweet butter (optional)
Cracked black pepper to taste
Chopped parsley for garnish

1. Heat oil in a skillet. Add the garlic, onion, and scallions, and let them "sweat"* about 6 minutes. Mix in olives and seasonings.

2. Raise heat, add chicken strips, and sauté for about 4 minutes. Place chicken mixture in a warm serving dish.

3. Deglaze skillet with vermouth and ½ cup of stock. Cook to reduce, adding additional stock if needed.

4. Enrich sauce with butter, if desired, and season with pepper. Pour over chicken, and garnish with parsley. *Serves 4.*

*Restaurant kitchen jargon, meaning to sauté through without browning.

Chicken Scarpariello

Scarpa means "shoe" in Italian. Legend has it that some beggars stole a couple of chickens, killed them with their shoes, then plucked, dressed, and cooked the birds on the spot. True or not, this is a dish fit for both beggars and kings. Italian bread and baked eggplant are fitting accompaniments.

PREPARATION TIME *10 minutes*
COOKING *30 minutes*

4 whole chicken legs (thighs and drumsticks)
1 cup oil
8 cloves of garlic, thickly sliced
¾ cup white wine
¾ cup chicken stock
1 lemon, halved, one half sliced
¼ cup chopped parsley

1. Wash chicken parts and dry with paper towels. Separate thighs from drumsticks. Heat oil in a deep skillet; add chicken. Sear pieces to a crisp, golden brown, about 3 minutes per side. Remove chicken to a separate dish and drain the fat from the pan.

2. Toss in the garlic and cook until brown and nutty. Return the chicken to the pan. Add the liquid; cook, uncovered, for about 20 to 25 minutes.

3. Squeeze the lemon half into the broth, then toss the lemon slices into pan and cook for another 3 minutes. Just before serving, add the chopped parsley. Spoon equal portions into individual soup bowls and serve. *Serves 4.*

Hint

Chopping chicken parts is best done with a cleaver, an indispensable tool in the kitchen.

Spicy Chicken Wings

This dish is economical as well as tasty. Crispy fried potato skins and a corn salad would fit right in.

MARINATING TIME *3 hours or overnight*
PREPARATION TIME *5 minutes*
COOKING *20 minutes*

Marinade

½ cup tomato sauce
2 tablespoons herb vinegar
¼ cup olive oil
2 cloves garlic, crushed
½ cup brown sugar
1 teaspoon celery seeds
6 peppercorns
Dash of Tabasco
½ teaspoon chili powder

16 to 24 chicken wings

1. Combine all the marinade ingredients and heat to a quick boil; let cool.
2. Submerge the chicken wings in marinade, cover, and refrigerate for a few hours, or overnight, turning the wings once.
3. When ready to cook, preheat broiler.
4. Arrange wings evenly over foil or in broiling pan. Brush with marinade and broil for about 10 minutes on each side, or until crispy. Check broiler often, lower rack if chicken starts to burn. Serve hot, or at room temperature. *Serves 4.*

Hint

Since I find it more economical to buy a whole chicken and cut it up myself, I always have plenty of wings. I store them in a plastic bag in the freezer and keep adding as I go along.

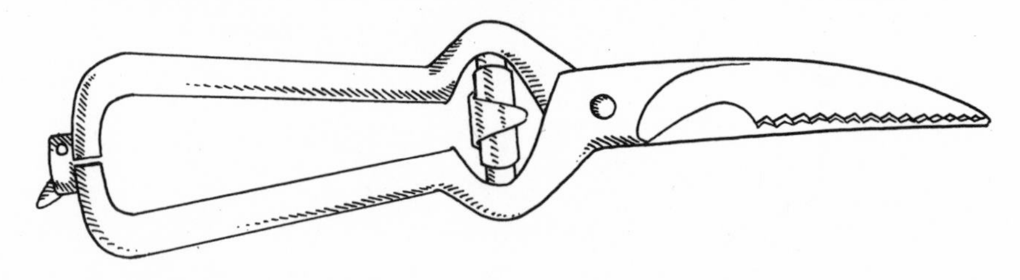

Smothered Chicken

This mild version of a curry is adapted from a recipe that my cousin, Ellen Less, gave me. It can be made ahead of time and refrigerated. Serve rice and mango chutney with it.

PREPARATION TIME *15 minutes*
COOKING *1 hour*

Two 2-pound chickens, cut into serving pieces, with skin removed
2 tablespoons flour
3 teaspoons oil
1 cup finely chopped onions
1 cup finely chopped celery
4 large apples, peeled, cored, and chopped
½ teaspoon paprika
¼ teaspoon ground ginger
¼ teaspoon ground turmeric
Pinch of cayenne
½ teaspoon black pepper
2 cups chicken stock, brought to a boil
½ cup shredded coconut

1. Dust the chicken pieces with flour. Heat the oil in a large skillet and brown the chicken pieces, about 5 minutes on each side. Remove and set aside.

2. Sauté the onions and celery until translucent. Add apples and seasonings, and cook for 15 minutes.

3. Return the chicken to the skillet, and add the stock. Reduce heat, cover, and let simmer for 30 minutes, or until chicken is tender. Before serving, sprinkle with coconut. *Serves 4.*

Hint

If you have 1 or 2 cups of cooked chicken left over, this is a good way to use it up. Make the sauce as directed, and add your chicken 15 minutes before serving.

4

Formal Lunches

IMPORTANT visitors, whether bent on business or pleasure, usually expect and deserve more formal midday dining, when the customary light lunch gives way to a more elaborate meal. The menu should be original and stimulating; presentation and service play important roles. So leave nothing to chance—it's best to prepare a dish that you are familiar with, for timing is vital.

Sautéed Medallions with Fresh Herbs

This dish can be made with a minimum of fuss, particularly if you chop all the ingredients ahead of time. Store the shallots and capers in separate covered containers in the refrigerator; combine the herbs and keep them covered. Individual molds of angel hair pasta and a side dish of marinated mushrooms make an impressive presentation.

PREPARATION TIME *15 minutes*
COOKING *6 to 7 minutes*

4 whole boneless and skinless chicken breasts, halved to make 8 fillets
White pepper
4 teaspoons butter
1 tablespoon oil
4 shallots, minced
¼ cup finely chopped fresh dill, stems removed
¼ cup finely chopped fresh tarragon leaves
¼ cup finely chopped fresh thyme
⅛ cup small capers, rinsed, drained, and chopped
¼ cup chicken broth
Juice of 1 lemon

1. To make the medallions, place fillets between 2 sheets of wax paper and pound lightly with a mallet or rolling pin. Trim each fillet to obtain 2 round or oval pieces. Pepper both sides and set aside for 10 minutes.

2. Heat 2 teaspoons butter in a skillet. When it begins to foam, add the medallions to the pan without crowding. (You may have to cook medallions in 2 batches.) Sauté for 1 minute on each side (the flesh should be white with just a touch of pink). Arrange the medallions on a warm serving platter and cover while preparing the sauce.

3. In the same skillet, heat the oil and sauté the shallots for 2 to 3 minutes. Add the herbs and sauté for 1 minute. Add the capers, chicken broth, and lemon juice, and swirl in the remaining 2 teaspoons of butter. Pour the sauce evenly over medallions and serve. *Serves 4.*

Hint

You can use dried instead of fresh herbs in this dish, although it won't taste the same. Dried herbs are stronger than fresh, so use only ½ teaspoon of each.

Poached Chicken with Saffron Rice

Saffron is the world's most costly spice. No wonder, considering that an estimated 75,000 to half a million flowers are necessary to produce one pound of saffron. Fortunately, only a small pinch of this pungent spice is needed in cooking.

Braised celery makes an excellent accompaniment to this dish.

PREPARATION TIME *20 minutes*
COOKING *1 hour and 45 minutes*

One 4-pound chicken
1 onion, peeled and studded with 2 cloves
2 carrots, peeled and quartered
2 cloves garlic
Bouquet Garni (see page 17)
1 cup white wine
1 quart chicken stock
Salt and white pepper to taste
1 tablespoon oil
1 onion, chopped
1¼ cups rice
Pinch of saffron, steeped in 1 to 2 tablespoons boiling water
Pinch of ground cumin
Grated Parmesan (optional)
Parsley for garnish

1. Truss the chicken as directed on page 6. Put the chicken into a 5-quart Dutch oven or stockpot with the onion, carrots, garlic, and bouquet garni. Add the wine and enough chicken stock to cover. Add some pepper and bring to a boil.

2. Reduce the heat, cover, and simmer for 1¼ to 1½ hours, or until tender, skimming off scum occasionally. Remove the chicken, and discard the trussing string. Let the chicken rest for 5 minutes before cutting it into 6 to 8 pieces.

3. Remove the skin, cover the chicken, and keep it in a warm place. Skim the excess fat from the cooking stock. Strain and boil until it is reduced by half. Taste for seasoning.

4. Heat the oil in a stove-top casserole dish or saucepan with a lid. Add the chopped onion and cook over a low flame until the onion is soft but not brown.

5. Add the rice, and stir over low flame until the rice becomes transparent. Add the reduced stock, saffron, and cumin. Cover, and simmer for 20 minutes, or until the rice is tender and has absorbed all the liquid. Remove from heat.

6. Stir the rice lightly with a fork and taste for seasoning. Add the chicken pieces, cover, and reheat briefly. Sprinkle with Parmesan, if desired. Garnish with parsley. Serve hot from the casserole. *Serves 4.*

Poultry Dumplings with Shiitake Mushrooms

A salad of endive, watercress, and roasted peppers would be a particularly eye-appealing accompaniment to this dish.

PREPARATION TIME *15 minutes*
COOKING *7 minutes*

2 whole boneless and skinless chicken breasts, about 1 pound
½ cup bread crumbs
1 cup skim milk
1 egg white
1 tablespoon chopped fresh oregano, or 1 teaspoon dried
1 tablespoon chopped fresh chives
Generous dash of nutmeg
Salt and freshly ground black pepper to taste
2 teaspoons butter
3 shallots, peeled and finely minced
½ pound fresh shiitake mushrooms, sliced
1 teaspoon flour
½ cup white wine
3 tablespoons finely chopped fresh dill

1. Cut the chicken into 1-inch cubes. Put the cubes in a food processor, blend thoroughly, and scrape chicken into a mixing bowl.

2. Soak the bread crumbs in milk and add to the chicken. Add egg white, oregano, chives, nutmeg, pepper, and salt, and mix well. Chill in the refrigerator for 15 minutes or longer.

3. With a tablespoon, form the chicken mixture into egg-shaped dumplings. Drop the dumplings into boiling salted water, reduce heat, and let them simmer for 5 to 7 minutes, until they begin to rise to the surface. With a slotted spoon, transfer the dumplings to a warm serving dish and set aside.

4. While the dumplings are simmering, heat the butter in a skillet and sauté the shallots for 3 minutes over medium heat. Add the mushrooms, and sauté over high heat. Sprinkle with flour, stirring a few times. Add the wine, and cook until thickened and slightly reduced to a nice consistency for a sauce. Season with plenty of pepper, and sprinkle in dill.

5. Drain the collected liquid from the serving dish, garnish the dumplings with mushroom sauce, and serve. *Serves 4.*

Roasted Butterflied Rock Cornish Hen

To butterfly is to split meat, fish, or fowl through the middle without completely separating the two halves, then to spread it out so that it resembles a butterfly. It takes imagination to see a hen as a butterfly, but the butterflying technique helps to produce an evenly cooked bird. It also makes an attractive presentation, which can be further enhanced by the addition of green asparagus with lemon sauce and braised brown rice.

PREPARATION TIME *25 minutes*
COOKING *35 minutes*

Four 1¼-pound Rock Cornish hens
Salt and pepper to taste
Sweet paprika to taste
2 teaspoons dried thyme
2 tablespoons oil
2 tablespoons butter
Watercress for garnish

1. Butterfly the hens as directed on page 10. Wipe dry, and season with salt, pepper, and paprika.

2. Preheat the oven to 400°F.

3. Heat oil and butter in a 12-inch ovenproof skillet. Brown the birds, skin side down first, for 8 minutes on each side.

4. Put into the preheated oven for about 15 minutes, turning once. Transfer to a serving dish and garnish with watercress. *Serves 4.*

Chicken Salad with Mango and Buttermilk Dressing

The exotic mango, a fruit with a combined tart-sweet flavor, is a native plant of India. Mango groves offer welcome shade and shelter to many brilliantly colored birds, and are a favorite destination for Indian families on a Sunday stroll.

Favorite accompaniments to this dish are toasted squares of pita bread and thin slices of chilled, peeled oranges.

PREPARATION TIME *25 minutes*
COOKING *50 minutes*

One 3½-pound chicken
2 mangoes, peeled, seeded, sliced 1 inch long and ½ inch thick
12 lychee nuts, quartered
2 sweet red peppers, cored, seeded, and cut into thin strips
2 small, firm red cabbages, halved, with centers scooped out to form 4 serving cups

Buttermilk Dressing

½ cup low-fat buttermilk
½ cup plain low-fat yogurt
1 teaspoon fresh orange juice
Juice of ½ lemon
1 teaspoon minced fresh dill
Pinch of ground cumin
Freshly ground black pepper to taste

Lettuce leaves for garnish
Sprigs of fresh mint or lemon verbena for decoration (optional)

1. Poach the chicken as directed on page 8. When the chicken is cool, remove the meat and discard the skin and bones. Cut the meat into even, bite-size portions.

2. Combine the prepared mangoes and lychee nuts with the chicken.

3. Drop the red pepper strips into boiling water for 1 minute. Drain, run briefly under cold water, dry on paper towels, and add to the chicken mixture. Set aside.

4. To make buttermilk dressing, combine all of the ingredients for the dressing, and shake well. Adjust seasoning and store, tightly covered, in the refrigerator.

5. When ready to serve, carefully add the dressing to the chicken mixture. Adjust seasoning again, and spoon into the prepared red cabbage containers. Set on carefully chosen lettuce greens and decorate with sprigs of fresh mint or lemon verbena. Serve at room temperature. *Serves 4.*

Hint

When selecting a mango, look for one with a thin, smooth skin and a reddish-yellow color.

Baked Chicken Roulades with Pesto

"Poultry is for the cook what canvas is for the painter," wrote Anthelme Brillat-Savarin, that much-quoted French gastronomic wit of the nineteenth century. Here is a dish that capitalizes on that maxim. Moreover, it's easily assembled, and better when prepared ahead of time—even the night before. Serve with brown basmati rice and grilled tomatoes.

PREPARATION TIME *20 minutes*
COOKING *25 minutes*

Pesto

2 large cloves garlic
2 tablespoons pine nuts
2 cups tightly packed fresh basil with stems removed
¼ cup chopped parsley
½ teaspoon salt
⅓ cup extra-virgin olive oil

4 whole boneless and skinless chicken breasts
½ cup finely ground bread crumbs
Pinch of freshly grated nutmeg
Pinch of salt
Watercress or parsley for garnish

1. To make the pesto, mince garlic and pine nuts in a blender or food processor. Add basil, parsley, and salt, and blend briefly. Add the oil in a steady stream while blending. Set aside.

2. Place each fillet between 2 sheets of wax paper, and flatten with a rolling pin or mallet.

3. Pat the fillets dry and spread 1½ tablespoons pesto over each portion. Starting at pointed edge, roll up fillets. Wrap each roulade in foil, and put it in the refrigerator for at least 20 minutes or overnight.

4. Preheat the oven to 350°F.

5. Remove foil from roulades and coat them lightly with bread crumbs mixed with the nutmeg and salt.

6. Place roulades on a baking sheet, and bake in preheated oven for 20 to 25 minutes. Remove them and let rest for 10 minutes.

7. Slice the roulades into ½-inch pieces and arrange them on a serving platter. Surround with watercress or parsley and serve. *Serves 4.*

Hint

Stored in a tightly covered jar, pesto will keep 2 weeks in the refrigerator and up to 6 months in the freezer.

Sautéed Suprêmes with Red Pepper Coulis

Coulis is the French term for a sauce obtained from the reduction of a blend of various ingredients. Our pepper coulis is a cold, thick sauce made from fresh vegetables and herbs, which adds spice to the classic chicken suprême. A nice accompaniment to the suprêmes would be cooked fava beans cooled to room temperature and flavored with lemon juice and garlic.

PREPARATION TIME *15 minutes*
COOKING *10–15 minutes*

Coulis

4 red peppers
2 tablespoons olive oil
¼ cup chopped fresh coriander, stems removed
4 shallots, peeled and minced
½ teaspoon ground cumin
Few drops of lemon juice
1 small clove garlic, crushed
¼ teaspoon salt

4 suprêmes, neatly trimmed (page 10)
2 teaspoons extra-virgin olive oil
1 teaspoon butter
Fresh pepper to taste
Sprigs of fresh mint for garnish

1. To make coulis, set peppers upright on open gas flame and rotate for 5 to 6 minutes to char, or if you have an electric stove, use the broiler, and broil peppers approximately 7 minutes per side to char. Drop the charred peppers into a bucket of ice water, then peel, clean, and core. Chop very fine. Slowly add the olive oil and the rest of the ingredients for the coulis to the peppers, and mix well. Store in a tightly covered jar until ready to use.

2. Dry the suprêmes with paper towels.

3. Heat the oil in a skillet, add the suprêmes, and sauté for 3 minutes. Add the butter and sauté for another 2 minutes. Pour fat out of the skillet, turn the suprêmes, and dry-sauté for 5 to 7 minutes, or until tender. Remove from the heat and season with pepper.

4. Equally divide the pepper coulis among 4 plates, and arrange the suprêmes on top. Garnish each plate with sprigs of fresh mint. *Serves 4.*

Warm Squab Salad

I prefer my squab slightly underdone, with a bit of pink showing. If you like a more well-done bird, increase the cooking time accordingly. This squab dish goes very well with a baguette and braised fennel.

PREPARATION TIME *5 minutes*
COOKING *30 to 35 minutes*

4 squabs
1 tablespoon oil
White pepper
3 tablespoons honey
4 tablespoons cider vinegar
½ teaspoon dried thyme
Chicory leaves for garnish

1. Preheat the oven to 450°F.
2. Rub the outsides of the squabs with oil, and season lightly with pepper. Place the squabs, breast side up, in a roasting pan just big enough to hold them.
3. Roast birds for 20 minutes, turn, and roast for another 10 minutes. Remove pan from the oven, then remove squabs from the pan and let them rest for 15 minutes.
4. Place the roasting pan over medium heat, stir in the honey, and cook until it begins to caramelize. Stir in the vinegar and thyme. Remove the pan from the heat and adjust seasoning.
5. Carve the squabs by separating wings and legs and entire breast section (slice the breast meat on the diagonal). Line a serving platter with chicory leaves, arrange the squab pieces over the chicory, and spoon sauce over the meat. *Serves 4.*

Chicken Escabèche

This is a piquant, jellied dish of Spanish origin, ideal for warm weather. It's easy to make, impressive to serve, and can be done ahead of time. Excellent served with spaghetti squash and seasonal vegetables.

PREPARATION TIME *10 minutes*
COOKING *35 minutes*
SETTING *4 hours or overnight*

3 cloves garlic, peeled and crushed
2 tablespoons lime juice
2 tablespoons lemon juice
¾ cup white wine
¼ cup cider vinegar
Bouquet garni of 2 bay leaves, 10 peppercorns, 10 mustard seeds, and 1 teaspoon dried thyme tied in cheesecloth
1 tablespoon oil
2 tablespoons imported small capers, rinsed and drained
4 whole chicken legs, drumsticks and thighs separated, skin removed
Chopped parsley for garnish
Thin slices of lemon or lime for garnish

1. Combine all the ingredients except the chicken, parsley, and lemon and lime slices in a large skillet, bring the mixture to a boil, reduce heat, and simmer for 10 minutes.

2. Add the chicken to the skillet, cover, and cook 25 to 30 minutes, turning chicken pieces over during cooking.

3. Remove from the heat, and allow to cool slightly. Remove the bouquet garni.

4. Arrange chicken in a deep serving dish. Pour liquid over all. Refrigerate and let set to jell. Serve cold, garnished with chopped parsley and thin lime or lemon slices. *Serves 4.*

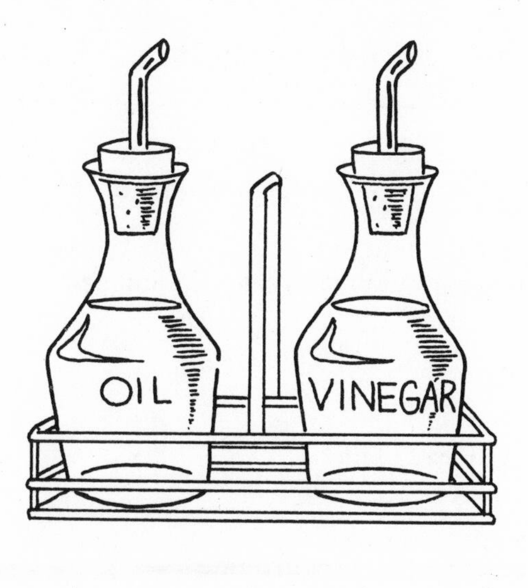

Hint

Efficiency, even in small matters, is part of restaurant kitchen management. Pourers (or spouts) on oil, vinegar, and cooking wine bottles help to speed up production, as does the handy tray set up with seasonings and garnishes. I have adopted that practice in my own kitchen at home; it is speedy, economical, and means fewer utensils to clean and put away.

Broiled Chicken in Orange Marinade

A simple accompaniment of broiled onion slices would make a delightful contrast to the complex flavors of this delicious dish.

PREPARATION TIME *25 minutes*
MARINATING *overnight*
COOKING *20 minutes*

2 small chickens, quartered, with wings removed

Marinade

8 cloves garlic, unpeeled
½ cup fresh grapefruit juice
½ cup fresh orange juice
¼ cup fresh lemon juice
Zest of one grapefruit
2 bay leaves, crushed
1 teaspoon dried rosemary
1 teaspoon dried marjoram
1 teaspoon dried thyme
1 teaspoon cracked pepper

Sauce

2 tablespoons balsamic vinegar
¼ cup honey
Salt and pepper to taste
Lettuce leaves (optional)
Chopped parsley for garnish

1. To make marinade, roast the garlic in a heavy skillet over medium heat, turning occasionally until slightly blackened and soft, about 15 minutes. When cool enough to handle, slip off the skins and mash to a paste. Combine with the remaining marinade ingredients.

2. Make a few deep cuts into the chicken to allow marinade to penetrate. Pour marinade over the chicken, cover, and refrigerate overnight, turning the chicken a few times.

3. When ready to use, preheat the broiler.

4. Place the chicken in the broiler pan, skin side up, remove the bay leaves from the marinade, and pour some of the marinade over the chicken. Broil for 10 minutes, then turn with tongs. Broil for another 10 minutes and remove white meat pieces to a platter. Broil dark meat for another 3 to 4 minutes, if needed, and add to platter.

5. Pour the remaining marinade into a skillet, and add the rendered juices from the broiled chicken. Add the balsamic vinegar and bring to a boil. Reduce heat, and slowly add honey, using a wooden spoon to stir. When the sauce begins to thicken, remove from the heat. Skim off any surface fat. Adjust seasoning.

6. Arrange the chicken on a serving platter, preferably on a bed of lettuce. Brush tops with the sauce, and serve the remaining sauce separately. Sprinkle with chopped parsley. *Serves 4.*

Picnics

TRADITIONALLY, a picnic is an open-air meal—dining al fresco. Today the term can apply to any portable meal. I have enjoyed picnics in the dead of winter, in front of a roaring fire. I have served a picnic on the bare floor of an empty apartment. And, not being overly fond of airline food, I usually travel with my own picnic basket on any flight over 5 hours long.

Summer Cornucopia

A cornucopia, a horn of plenty overflowing with fruit and ears of grain, is a symbol of abundance. No grains in this dish, but plenty of summer fruits, for that special picnic.

PREPARATION TIME *30 minutes*
COOKING *45 minutes*

*One 3½-pound chicken**
½ cup hulled and washed blueberries
½ cup hulled, washed, and halved strawberries
2 medium-size cucumbers, peeled, with seeds removed
1 tart apple, cored and cut into small cubes
Juice of ½ lemon
½ teaspoon salt
1 cup mayonnaise
4 small, ripe melons
1 kiwi, peeled, cut into ¼-inch slices, and quartered

1. Poach the chicken as directed on page 8. Remove the skin and bones, tear into large, even chunks, and combine with berries, cucumbers, and apple.

2. Add lemon juice and salt to mayonnaise. Pour over the salad and mix carefully. Adjust seasoning.

3. The chicken salad will be served in melon baskets. To prepare the baskets, stand up a melon. With a sharp knife, define and cut handle midway down the melon. Define and cut deep crown on both sides of handle. Carefully scoop out flesh of melon, until it is almost hollow. Drain off any excess liquid and store baskets in the refrigerator until ready to use.

4. When ready to serve, divide chicken salad among the 4 baskets and decorate with kiwi fruit. *Serves 4.*

*Leftover chicken can be used in this recipe.

Chicken Burgers

This burger deliciously upstages the ubiquitous hamburger. Nevertheless, serve it with the traditional cole slaw and rolls.

PREPARATION TIME *15 minutes*
COOKING *8 minutes*

1 small onion, chopped fine
1 tablespoon butter
½ cup skim milk, warmed
2 slices stale white bread, broken in pieces
1 pound raw chicken, ground
1 teaspoon dried thyme
8 black olives, pitted and finely chopped
1 tablespoon finely chopped parsley
½ teaspoon white pepper
1 cup unflavored bread crumbs
1 tablespoon oil

1. Sauté the onion in the butter until wilted. Set aside.
2. Combine the milk and bread, and mix until smooth. Add the ground chicken, sautéed onion, thyme, and olives, and mix well. (If the texture is too thick, add more milk.)
3. Shape into 2-inch patties.
4. Mix the parsley and white pepper into the bread crumbs. Dip chicken patties into the bread-crumb mixture to coat.
5. Heat the oil in a skillet. Sauté the patties, about 3 minutes on each side. *Serves 4.*

Rock Cornish Hen with Grilled Vegetables

This dish is eminently suitable for an elegant picnic, complete with champagne and your best silver. A dandelion salad and grilled potato slices are appropriate accompaniments.

PREPARATION TIME *15 minutes*
MARINATING *1 hour*
COOKING *30 minutes*

4 Rock Cornish hens
Juice of 2 lemons
1 tablespoon oil
2 teaspoons finely chopped fresh rosemary leaves, or 1 teaspoon dried
2 red peppers, seeded and cut into strips
4 small zucchini, washed and sliced
2 teaspoons finely chopped fresh thyme leaves, or 1 teaspoon dried

1. Cut the Cornish hens down the back, press flat, remove the backbones, and marinate in the lemon juice, oil, and rosemary mixture for about 1 hour.

2. Preheat grill.

3. Put the hens on the grill, bone side down, and grill for a total of 30 minutes, turning them occasionally to avoid burning. Baste with the marinade. Add the peppers and zucchini, and grill for 5 to 8 minutes. Arrange hens on platter and surround with vegetables. Sprinkle with thyme and serve. *Serves 4.*

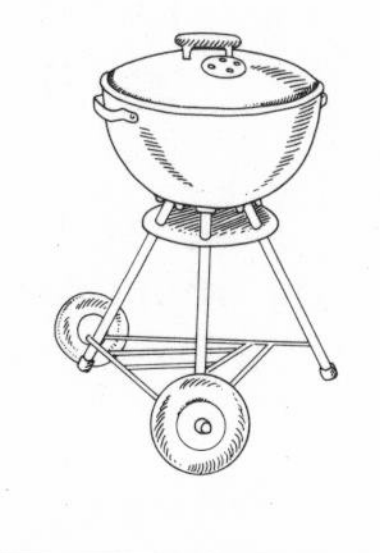

Hint

It usually takes about 45 minutes for the charcoal to become hot enough for proper barbecuing. You can also add mesquite chips, fruit wood, or sprigs of pine to the coals to enhance the flavor of the meat.

Curried Chicken

In India, the use of premixed curry powder is much frowned upon, partly because freshly ground spices are infinitely more aromatic, and partly because different dishes call for different proportions of spices. Occasionally, Indians may use a mixture of spices called *garam masala,* meaning "hot mixture." A garam masala might consist of a carefully balanced blend of roasted coriander seed, roasted chili, and black pepper ground very fine and then stored in a tin with a closely fitted lid. Certain stores carry premixed garam masala, but it is as convenient, and more authentic, to make your own "hot mixture." Serve this delicious curry with chutney and toasted coconut.

PREPARATION TIME *5 minutes*
COOKING *12 minutes*

2 whole boneless and skinless chicken breasts, halved and flattened
1 teaspoon oil
1 teaspoon butter
¼ cup balsamic vinegar
½ cup white wine
1 tablespoon oil

1 cup light mayonnaise
Lemon or grape leaves, if available
Banana and mango for garnish

Garam Masala

¼ teaspoon ground black pepper
¼ teaspoon cayenne
2½ teaspoons ground coriander
1 tablespoon ground turmeric

1. Trim and dry the chicken breasts with paper towels.
2. Heat the oil and butter in a skillet, and sauté the chicken breasts 4 minutes on one side and 3 minutes on the other. Set aside.
3. In a saucepan, combine the vinegar, wine, and oil with the garam masala mixture and any excess juices from chicken. Boil rapidly over high heat to reduce.
4. When it has slightly cooled, combine the mixture with the mayonnaise.
5. Slice the chicken breasts on the diagonal and place on a bed of lemon or grape leaves, if available. Garnish with mango and banana slices. Serve the sauce separately. *Serves 4.*

Oven-Barbecued Chicken for a Crowd

This crowd pleaser calls for a tasty barbecue sauce that should be made ahead of time. It will keep in the refrigerator for up to a week or so.

Serve this dish with dirty rice and pickled onions.

PREPARATION TIME *25 minutes*
COOKING *1 hour and 20 minutes*

Barbecue Sauce

6 cloves garlic, chopped
½ onion, chopped
One 1-pound can pineapple, chopped, with juice
¼ cup lemon juice
¾ cup ginger ale
1 quart ketchup
1 cup prepared mustard
2 teaspoons chili powder
2 teaspoons ground cumin
2 teaspoons black pepper
1 teaspoon white pepper
Dash of Tabasco
1 cup honey (optional)

½ cup flour
1 teaspoon chili powder
1 teaspoon cayenne pepper
1 teaspoon ground cumin
Five 3½-pound chickens, each cut into 6 pieces
½ cup oil

1. To make barbecue sauce, soak the first 3 ingredients in saucepan for 5 minutes. Add the lemon juice and ginger ale, and cook until sauce is reduced by half. Add remaining ingredients, and simmer for 40 to 50 minutes. Adjust the seasoning according to taste.
2. Preheat the oven to 400°F.
3. Mix the flour and spices, and dust chicken parts.
4. Coat a large roasting pan or 2 smaller pans with oil and place in the preheated oven. When pans are heated, add the chicken pieces and sear them for 15 minutes; turn and sear other side for another 15 minutes, or until brown.
5. Spoon the sauce over the chicken. Reduce oven to 325°F., and roast the chicken for 45 minutes or so, until just before the meat starts to fall off the bone, turning chicken once. Serve directly from roasting pan. *Serves 20.*

Baked Wingsticks

The celebrated food writer M. F. K. Fisher recalls that on the occasion of her father's seventy-fifth birthday, the family served him 75 chicken wings. The gesture was not appreciated. Her father did not object to the chicken wings—he just objected to being reminded of his age!

Serve with potato salad.

PREPARATION TIME *at least 1½ hours*
COOKING *15 minutes*

75 chicken wings, the first or middle joints only

Flour, seasoned with salt, pepper, and paprika
½ cup vegetable oil

1. Preheat the oven to 400°F.
2. Cut around the edge of bottom joint to loosen the tendons. When free, push meat from the top down to the bottom of the joint. As you push, the meat descends and the skin turns in automatically—push this over the knuckle to form a ball (see drawing).

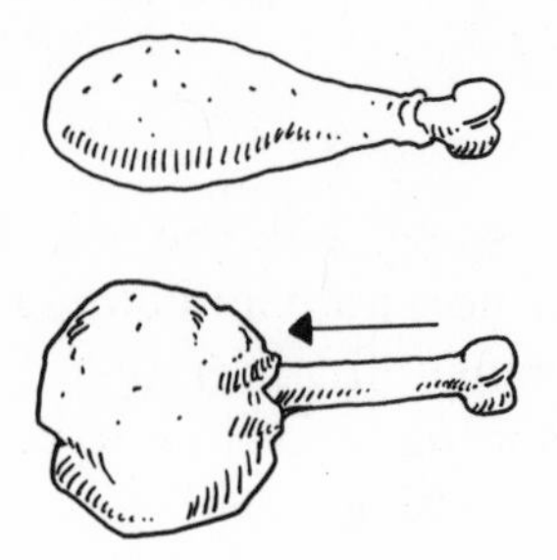

3. Flour the wings lightly. Heat the oil in a large skillet and brown the wings for 5 minutes or so. Arrange them on a baking sheet, put in the preheated oven for about 10 minutes, until crisp. Serve with your favorite barbecue sauce, or a grainy mustard. *Serves a crowd.*

Hint

This is messy fun food, meant to be eaten out-of-doors. Make sure to have plenty of paper napkins and a garbage bag handy.

Bistro Salad

I call this a bistro salad because the white beans and the raw red beets remind me of some of the savory salad dishes I have tasted in French and Belgian bistros over the years. Serve with crusty French bread and a bowl of radishes.

PREPARATION TIME *15 minutes*
SOAKING *overnight*
COOKING *1 hour and 20 minutes*

½ pound Great Northern beans
*1 large chicken breast, halved**
3 cups plus 2 tablespoons chicken stock
1 stalk dried sage
2 bay leaves
2 cloves garlic, peeled
2 teaspoons chopped green onions
½ cup extra-virgin olive oil
Juice of 1 lemon
1 teaspoon ground sage
Freshly ground black pepper
Outer leaves of red or savoy cabbage for lining
2 small fresh beets, peeled and cut into 1-inch strips
Chopped parsley for garnish

1. Cover beans with cold water and let them soak overnight.
2. Poach the chicken breast as directed on page 8, let cool, remove skin and bones, and set aside.
3. Drain the beans, place them in a large pot, add 3 cups of chicken stock, sage stalk, bay leaves, and garlic. Bring to a slow boil, cover, and let simmer over lowest possible heat for 1 hour. Test for doneness (beans should be slightly *al dente*).
4. Drain the beans, discard bay leaves, sage, and garlic. Rinse the beans under cold water, and place them in a large bowl. Tear or cut the chicken into thin strips, and add to the bowl together with green onions.
5. In a small saucepan, beat the oil into the lemon juice, add 2 tablespoons chicken stock, whisk in the sage, and heat briefly without bringing to a boil.
6. Pour the warm dressing over the beans and chicken, add fresh pepper, and blend carefully. Adjust seasoning, adding more lemon juice if necessary. Line a serving platter with cabbage leaves and spoon salad into leaves, sprinkle with strips of red beet, and top with chopped parsley. *Serves 4.*

*Leftover chicken can be used in this recipe.

Chicken Legs Cajun Style

This is a spicy dish with a Southwestern kick. To complete the effect, serve with salsa and refried rice.

PREPARATION TIME *13 minutes*
COOKING *35 to 40 minutes*

1 egg yolk
1 tablespoon milk
4 whole chicken legs (thighs and drumsticks)
2 tablespoons bread crumbs
1 teaspoon flour
1 tablespoon freshly crushed black peppercorns
1 teaspoon white pepper
1 teaspoon paprika
1 teaspoon dried oregano
1 teaspoon chili powder
1 teaspoon allspice
1 teaspoon dried coriander
1 teaspoon dried sage
2 tablespoons oil
1 tablespoon butter
Lemon wedges for garnish

1. Beat the egg yolk with the milk and brush evenly over chicken legs.

2. Blend the remaining ingredients, except oil and butter, together, and dredge the chicken well in this mixture.

3. Heat the oil and butter in a large skillet. Add the chicken and brown all of it over high heat. Reduce heat to medium-low and sauté until cooked through, about 30 minutes. Serve with lemon wedges. *Serves 4.*

Hint

Freshly crushed peppercorns have a totally different flavor from ground pepper. Try the old restaurant trick of putting a few whole peppercorns on a flat surface and crushing them with the rim of a soup bowl. Or use a mallet, if it is more convenient.

Boned Legs with Roasted Pepper and Mushroom Filling

These legs travel well. They make excellent picnic fare when placed in pita bread and eaten out of hand. A pasta salad is a good accompaniment.

PREPARATION TIME *45 minutes*
COOKING *35 minutes*

4 whole chicken legs (thighs and drumsticks)
1 tablespoon olive oil
¼ cup minced green onions
⅓ cup chopped roasted red peppers
1 cup chopped mushrooms
2 tablespoons bread crumbs
½ teaspoon vinegar
2 teaspoons chopped fresh dill

1. Preheat the oven to 350°F.
2. Bone the chicken legs as directed on page 11.
3. Heat the olive oil in a large skillet, and sauté the onions, peppers, and mushrooms. Add the bread crumbs, vinegar, and dill, and mix well.
4. Place one-fourth of the filling in the center of each leg. Fold flaps of leg meat over the filling, forming a package. Place each stuffed leg in the center of a piece of oiled 5-inch-square aluminum foil, and wrap it well. Place the packages on a baking sheet, and put into the preheated oven.
5. Bake for 25 minutes. Remove the packages from the oven, raise heat to broil, open each package, and put under the broiler for 5 minutes to brown the tops. *Serves 4.*

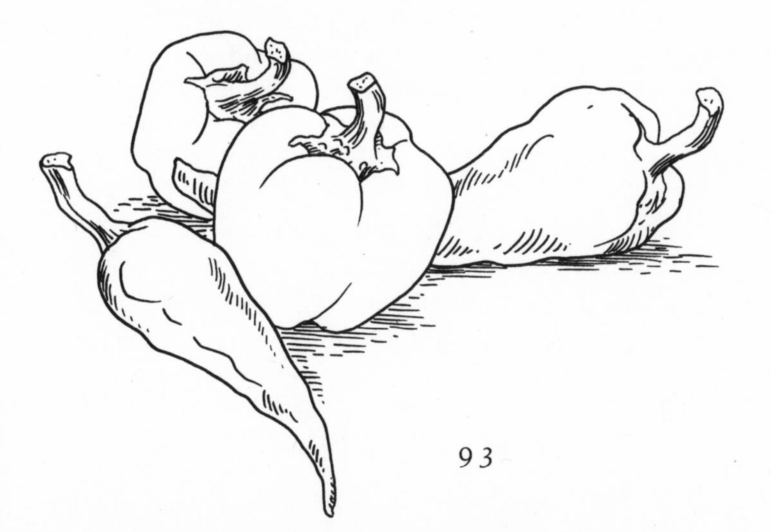

Crispy Chicken with Garlic and Rosemary

Picnics require that the food can be easily carried and eaten without too much fuss—everything in bite-size portions. Fingers are ideal utensils for this type of fare. Since a third of the world's population eats with its fingers, maintaining that this is the only way really to savor the texture and the flavor of the food, why should we object? The following picnic dish is a case in point. Serve with caponata and marinated mushrooms.

PREPARATION TIME *20 minutes*
COOKING *1 hour and 20 minutes*

One 4-pound chicken
4 cloves garlic, peeled and sliced
1 tablespoon dried rosemary
½ teaspoon salt
1 tablespoon butter, softened
Oil
Salt and pepper to taste

1. Preheat the oven to 400°F.
2. Clean the bird and pat it dry. Loosen the skin carefully, and insert garlic slivers and 1½ teaspoons rosemary under the skin. Sprinkle the cavity with salt.
3. Mash the rest of the rosemary into the softened butter to form a ball, and place that in the body cavity. Rub the outside of the chicken with oil, and truss as directed on page 6.
4. Place chicken, breast side up, on the rack of a roasting pan, and put into the preheated oven. Roast for 20 minutes, turn it over, and roast the other side for 20 minutes. Turn it again, and prick the skin with a fork to allow fat to escape. Roast for another 20 minutes. Repeat process with the other side, roasting for an additional 15 minutes.
5. Remove the chicken, discard the accumulated fat, and let it rest for 15 minutes.*
6. Preheat the broiler. Remove the trussing string and cut the chicken into small parts with poultry shears.
7. Place dark meat pieces, skin side up, on broiling pan and broil for 2 minutes. Add white meat and broil for an additional 3 minutes.

8. Remove, season with salt and pepper to taste, and cool. Pile chicken pieces into an attractive basket and take on your picnic. *Serves 4.*

*Recipe may be made in advance up to this point.

Hint

It never fails—no sooner do I decide to make this dish, than the temperature shoots into the 90s. That's why I prefer to do the roasting on the evening before. Giving the roasted bird an overnight rest also helps to tighten the meat and makes it easier to cut for quick broiling.

6

Suppers for Two

SUPPER to me is the ultimate adult meal—a late repast shared by a few people, perhaps after an evening's entertainment, or by a couple enjoying the quiet and privacy of a special evening together. With this in mind, I have placed several of the choicest recipes in this chapter—dishes that call for an accompanying champagne or a fine wine. But since drinking champagne and cooking over a hot stove don't go together, these dishes may be prepared well ahead of time, requiring only a few last-minute touches.

Of course, there are those frantic days when supper chic is the furthest from one's mind. Then you want a meal that all but cooks itself, yet is savory enough to soothe a tired body and refresh sagging spirits. Some of the recipes included here are in that category. Since supper, plain or fancy, is to me still an intimate occasion, all the recipes in this chapter are meant for two persons.

Chicken Fillets in Parsley Aspic

Easy to make, this dish will wait for you. Offer it with a combination of sautéed onions and potatoes.

PREPARATION TIME *15 minutes*
COOKING *15 to 20 minutes*
RESTING *4 hours to overnight*

2 whole boneless and skinless chicken breasts
White pepper
2 teaspoons oil
2 teaspoons butter
2 cups chicken stock
1 package gelatin
¼ cup tarragon vinegar
1 egg white, lightly beaten
1 teaspoon Madeira (optional)
1 cup finely chopped parsley
1 clove garlic, peeled and thinly sliced
1 carrot, parboiled, sliced into an attractive shape for garnish
4 cornichons, sliced fanlike for garnish

1. Divide each breast into 2 fillets and trim. Dry the fillets and season with pepper.

2. Heat the oil and butter in a skillet. Sauté the fillets for 4 to 5 minutes on each side. Remove and set aside.

3. Bring the stock to a boil. Dissolve the gelatin in the vinegar, and add the mixture to the stock, bring to a boil, stirring. Reduce heat. To clarify stock, add beaten egg white to it, and stir with a wooden spoon. Let simmer gently for 10 minutes.

4. Line a sieve with a paper towel and strain the aspic through it (you may have to change paper towels a few times). Add the optional Madeira.

5. Coat the bottom of a large mold, or individual molds, with the aspic. Sprinkle with one-fourth of the parsley and allow to set slightly. Arrange the fillets over the aspic.

6. Garnish with the vegetables and sprinkle with the rest of the parsley. Cover with the remaining aspic, and put into the refrigerator to set. Serve in its own mold, or unmold it onto a platter. *Serves 2.*

Braised Chicken and Leek Birds

The leek is the national emblem of Wales. On St. David's Day, Welshmen wear a bit of leek in their buttonholes in memory of their victory over the Saxons.

Sautéed polenta and grilled tomato halves add a festive touch to this interesting dish.

PREPARATION TIME *20 minutes*
COOKING *23 minutes*

1 leek, trimmed, thoroughly washed, and cut in quarters lengthwise
Salt and freshly crushed peppercorns
2 whole boneless and skinless chicken breasts
1 tablespoon flour
1 tablespoon olive oil
¼ cup chicken stock
¼ cup white wine
½ lemon, quartered
1½ tablespoons chopped parsley
1½ tablespoons capers, drained and rinsed
Thin lemon slices or twists for garnish

1. Preheat the broiler.
2. Blanch the leek in boiling water, approximately 3 minutes. Drain, and season each length of leek with salt and pepper. Place them under the broiler for 2 minutes.
3. Divide each breast into 2 fillets and trim. Lay the leek pieces flat over the fillets, and roll them lengthwise, securing each with 2 toothpicks. Flour lightly.
4. Heat the olive oil in a large skillet. Brown "birds" evenly on both sides for about 7 to 8 minutes. Remove and set aside.
5. Add the stock and wine to the skillet, then squeeze the lemon quarters and drop them into the liquid. Bring to a slow boil.
6. Return the birds to the skillet and cook over moderate heat for about 10 minutes, turning occasionally.
7. Remove the chicken from the skillet and arrange it on a serving platter. Remove the toothpicks. Raise the heat, and add parsley and capers to sauce in skillet. Adjust the seasoning, then pour sauce over the birds and garnish the tops with thin slices of lemon. *Serves 2.*

Chicken Legs Baked over Slices of Orange and Sweet Onion

John Evelyn, a seventeenth-century English poet, sang the virtues of sage: " 'Tis a plant with so many properties ... that it is said to render men immortal."

Sage's power extends right into the kitchen, where its strong fragrance enhances any dish to which it is added. This particular dish goes well with lima beans and pimientos.

PREPARATION TIME *10 minutes*
COOKING *40 minutes*

1 tablespoon oil
2 whole chicken legs, thighs and drumsticks attached
3 teaspoons fresh sage, or 1 teaspoon dried
1 orange, cut into ½-inch slices
1 large sweet onion, cut into ½-inch slices
Salt and pepper to taste
¼ cup chicken stock

1. Preheat the oven to 375°F.

2. Heat a skillet and coat the bottom with oil. Add the legs, skin side down, and sear 3 to 4 minutes on each side. Toss sage into the skillet and heat through.

3. Arrange the orange slices in a baking dish and cover with the onion slices. Place legs on top, and sprinkle with the heated sage. Season with salt and pepper. Deglaze pan drippings with stock, and pour sauce over all.

4. Put the dish into the preheated oven, and bake for 35 to 40 minutes. *Serves 2.*

Poached Ballotine with Mushrooms and Fresh Marjoram

This is a very elegant dish and, like any work of art, takes time to prepare. Since the dish can be made well ahead of time, the effort is well worth it. Cold leeks with purée of tomatoes, also made ahead, complements this superb dish.

PREPARATION TIME *45 minutes*
COOKING *45 minutes*

One 2½-pound chicken
½ cup dried shiitake mushrooms
1 teaspoon oil
2 shallots, minced
1 teaspoon dry sherry
1 teaspoon chopped fresh marjoram
White pepper and salt to taste
Chicken stock to cover, about 3 cups

1. Bone the chicken as directed on page 12. Remove the legs, bone them, then cut the dark meat into small chunks and set aside.
2. Soak the mushrooms in hot water for 15 minutes, rinse them, and reserve the liquid. Chop the mushrooms.
3. Heat the oil in a skillet, and sauté shallots until translucent. Add the mushrooms, and sauté for 3 minutes, then add the sherry. Season with marjoram and white pepper and salt to taste, then set aside to cool.
4. Blend the reserved leg meat in a food processor for about 2 minutes. Add chicken meat to the shallot-and-mushroom mixture, together with enough mushroom liquid to obtain a smooth consistency.
5. Prepare the bird for stuffing by flattening out the skin. Spoon the stuffing mixture into the middle of the bird. Place the breast directly on top and fold over both sides of skin. Tuck the wing bones under. Fold double a piece of cheesecloth large enough to enclose the chicken and wrap it around the bird. Twist the ends and tie them off with twine.
6. Bring the stock to a boil, then reduce to a simmer. Gently lower the ballotine into the stock and let it poach, covered, for 22 to 25 minutes. Remove and let cool before unwrapping. *Serves 2.*

Hint

This dish is best served at room temperature, presented whole, or precut into 1-inch slices. Ballotines will keep in the refrigerator for up to 2 days.

Sauté of Chicken over Fresh Pasta with White Truffle Shavings

White truffles grow in the Piedmont area of northern Italy, where they appear on the market by late October. Their aroma is pungent and unmistakable. Once, walking in a Milanese market, I was suddenly struck by a strange odor. Following my nose, I came upon a tiny stall where a number of people were standing in line. A farmer was weighing some ugly-looking roots on a scale. "Trifolau, trifolau," he shouted. Later that evening at dinner, I encountered my first white truffle—a sensational gastronomic experience—which was followed by shock when I received the bill. It was worth it then; it is worth it now, particularly when shared with an intimate friend.

PREPARATION TIME *20 minutes*
MARINATING *4 hours*
COOKING *8 minutes*

2 cloves garlic, crushed
½ teaspoon salt
12 black peppercorns, crushed
⅓ cup olive oil
½ teaspoon dried tarragon
1 whole skinless and boneless chicken breast, cut into 1-inch cubes
½ pound mushrooms, preferably porcini or shiitake, cleaned and sliced
6 ounces fresh green pasta
Freshly ground pepper
Fresh tarragon leaves for garnish
1 small white truffle

1. Combine the garlic, salt, crushed peppercorns, and olive oil to make marinade. Heat the dried tarragon for 1 minute to bring up its flavor, then add to the marinade.
2. Place the chicken cubes and mushrooms in this mixture to marinate for about 4 hours.
3. Heat a skillet, preferably Teflon or iron, and quick-sauté the chicken and mushrooms (which will have soaked up almost all of the marinade), for about 5 minutes, tossing frequently.
4. Meanwhile, bring a big pot of water to a boil and add the pasta, cook for 2 minutes, and drain.

5. Put the pasta in a deep serving dish. Adjust seasoning of the chicken and mushroom mixture and toss with the pasta. Grind fresh pepper on it and decorate with tarragon leaves. Bring immediately to the table with the truffle. Shave truffle over each portion. *Serves 2.*

Hint

Boil the water for the pasta before cooking chicken pieces and mushrooms. Cook the pasta during the last 2 minutes of sautéing—so everything is done at the same time.

Chicken Puttanesca

The basic idea behind a puttanesca is to toss anything you have on hand into the pot, cook it, and then serve it in deep soup bowls with additional liquid, if desired. The dish may be prepared in advance, refrigerated, and then reheated. Serve with spaghetti.

PREPARATION TIME *40 minutes*
COOKING *30 minutes*

One 2½-pound chicken, cut into small serving pieces
Salt and pepper to taste
1 tablespoon oil
2 cloves garlic, finely sliced
1 small red onion, finely chopped
1 cup chicken stock
½ cup red or white wine
3 tomatoes, cut into ½-inch chunks, or a 1-pound can whole tomatoes
1½ tablespoons capers, rinsed and drained
6 black olives, pitted and chopped
6 green olives, pitted and chopped
1½ teaspoons basil leaves, chopped, or 1 teaspoon dried
1 teaspoon dried rosemary

1. Season the chicken pieces with salt and pepper. Heat a large skillet, add the oil, raise the heat, and sear the chicken, skin side down first, 5 to 7 minutes on each side. When nicely browned, remove and set aside.

2. Drain the oil, toss in the garlic and onion, and brown lightly. Add half of the stock, wine, and liquid from the canned tomatoes, the capers, and the olives, and warm through.

3. Return the chicken to the skillet, along with the diced tomatoes and the seasonings, and mix well. Add the remaining liquid to the skillet. Cook for another 15 minutes at a simmer, and serve. *Serves 2.*

Warm Oriental Chicken Salad

This salad has so much zip, it's hard to believe how quickly it can be tossed together. It's perfect served with Chinese rice noodles.

PREPARATION TIME *10 minutes*
COOKING *6 minutes*

Dressing

¼ cup rice vinegar
1½ teaspoons brown sugar
1 teaspoon soy sauce
Dash of Tabasco

*2 whole boneless and skinless chicken breasts, cut into ½-inch strips**
2 teaspoons flour
⅛ cup oil
½ cup julienned carrots
¼ cup finely chopped scallions
¼ teaspoon hot pepper flakes
1 teaspoon sesame seeds
½ cup drained bamboo shoots
Salt and pepper to taste

1. Mix the dressing ingredients together in a small saucepan over low heat. Just before the dressing begins to simmer, remove and set aside.

2. Dust the chicken strips lightly with flour. Heat the oil in a skillet or wok, and sauté chicken strips for 2 minutes on each side. Pour off fat.

3. Add the remaining ingredients, and sauté for 2 minutes, tossing frequently. Check the chicken for doneness and adjust seasoning. Remove the chicken and vegetables from the skillet, and arrange on a platter. Add warm dressing and serve. *Serves 2.*

*Use leftover chicken in this recipe, if desired.

Roasted Rock Cornish Hen with Black Currant Sauce

This is a dish with an exciting flavor combination. Glazed shallots would make an excellent accompaniment.

PREPARATION TIME *10 minutes*
MARINATING *4 hours or overnight*
COOKING *32 minutes*

2 Rock Cornish hens
Black pepper
1 teaspoon butter
1 teaspoon oil

Marinade

2 tablespoons oil
2 tablespoons lemon juice
Grated zest of 1 lemon
1 teaspoon dried thyme

Sauce

2 tablespoons red wine vinegar
¼ cup red wine
1 cup brown stock (page 18) or canned beef consommé
3 tablespoons black currant jam
Black pepper to taste
1 tablespoon butter

1. Split the hens in half, remove backbones, and season with pepper.
2. Make the marinade and marinate the hens for 4 hours or overnight. When ready to use, bring hens to room temperature.
3. Preheat the oven to 375°F.
4. Heat the oil and butter in a skillet. Remove hens from marinade, and sauté, skin side down first, for 5 minutes on each side, or until brown.
5. Place the hens in the preheated oven, and roast for 10 to 12 minutes on each side, until cooked through.
6. Meanwhile prepare the sauce by deglazing the skillet with vinegar and wine. Add the stock and boil rapidly to reduce. Lower the heat, add the black currant jam plus any pan drippings from the roasted hens.
7. Adjust the seasoning and, at the last minute, add the butter to the sauce and stir. Arrange the hens on a serving platter and spoon the sauce over them. *Serves 2.*

Hint

When grating orange or lemon peel, place a piece of wax paper behind the holes of a hand grater. Hold the wax paper in place with one hand and grate the fruit with the other hand. The grated zest will cling to the wax paper rather than to the surface of the grater.

Ropa Vieja

I was brought up in a household where wasting food was considered close to a crime. So throwing away good food is, to me, not just thoughtless, but uneconomical and unimaginative—much better to transform yesterday's feast into today's meal. My husband, who spent part of his childhood in Cuba, introduced me to this dish. Traditionally made with a less expensive cut of meat, the name means literally "old clothes." I never forgot the flavor: feisty, slightly sweet and sour. It's a tasty way to use up that leftover chicken, and goes wonderfully with rice and beans.

PREPARATION TIME *10 minutes*
COOKING *10 minutes*

1 tablespoon oil
2 shallots, peeled and chopped
1 clove garlic, minced
1 medium roasted red pepper, cut into strips
6 green olives, pitted and cut into chunks
2 bay leaves
1 cup leftover cooked chicken meat, cut into strips
1 teaspoon sugar
1 teaspoon mild vinegar
1 teaspoon white vermouth
Black pepper to taste

1. Heat the oil in a skillet and sauté shallots, garlic, pepper, olives, and bay leaves for 5 minutes. Remove with a slotted spoon and set aside.

2. Toss the chicken into the skillet, and sauté briefly. Raise the heat and sprinkle on the sugar to coat. Add the vinegar, vermouth, and pepper, and stir.

3. Return the shallot mixture to the skillet, and mix well. Remove the bay leaves and adjust the seasoning. Serve at once. *Serves 2.*

Pullao with Yogurt-Marinated Chicken

Although pilaf was born in Turkey, this rice dish has been adapted by many countries simply by adding different ingredients. Since this pilaf has some Indian characteristics, we call it by its Indian name, *pullao.*

PREPARATION TIME *20 minutes*
MARINATING *12 hours*
COOKING *25 minutes*

*2 cups boneless and skinless chicken meat, either breast or thigh**
2 teaspoons butter

Marinade

4 tablespoons plain low-fat yogurt
2 tablespoons oil
2 cloves garlic, peeled and crushed
Juice of 1 lemon or lime
½ teaspoon chili powder
½ teaspoon cayenne
2 teaspoons sweet paprika

Pullao

2 teaspoons oil
1 large onion, peeled and cut into rings
¾ cup long-grain rice
Grated zest of ¼ lemon
Pinch of cinnamon
2 bay leaves
Approximately 1½ cups boiling chicken stock
½ cup yellow raisins, softened in warm water and drained
White pepper to taste

1. Combine all the marinade ingredients.
2. Place the chicken in a container just large enough to hold it, and pour marinade over. Cover, and refrigerate for about 12 hours, turning the chicken once or twice.
3. Heat the oil for pullao in a skillet. Sauté the onion for about 4 minutes, or until brown, remove, and set aside.
4. Add the rice to the skillet, sauté for 3 minutes to coat. Add the lemon zest, cinnamon, and bay leaves, and enough stock for the rice to absorb, and stir. Add the raisins and cook, adding liquid as needed, until rice is tender, about 20 minutes. Remove the bay leaves, and adjust seasoning.

5. While the rice is simmering, scrape the marinade from the chicken, and reserve it in a small skillet.

6. Ten minutes before the rice is cooked, heat the butter in a medium-size skillet until foaming. Add the chicken, and sauté over high heat for about 4 minutes on each side, tossing frequently. Check for doneness (the marinated chicken will be as soft as butter), and do not overcook.

7. Cook reserved marinade over low heat for 1 or 2 minutes, or until slightly thickened.

8. Arrange the rice in a mound on a warm serving platter. Pile the chicken in the center, and pour the sauce over it. Surround the chicken with rings of cooked onion, and serve. *Serves 2.*

*Leftover chicken may be used in this recipe.

Hint

If you use leftover cooked chicken in this recipe, cut it into bite-size portions at room temperature, spike it with ground turmeric, and garnish it with paprika. Neither the texture nor the flavor will be quite the same, but the effect is similar.

Seasonal Meals

When I was a small child growing up in Europe, the coming and going of the seasons played a major part in my family's daily activities, as well as dictating what foods would appear on our dinner table. Spring meant white asparagus, pink rhubarb, and brown morels; summer brought fresh herbs, carrots, cucumbers, eggplant, and every kind of berry; autumn summoned forth peppers of astonishing colors, tart apples, and mellow pears; with early snow came cabbage, kale, and mustard greens.

I have never quite gotten over my reluctance to use produce out of season. It simply isn't the same. Luckily, chicken is always in season, and what fun to prepare it with fresh vegetables and fruits as soon as they appear in our markets, backyards, or gardens!

Baked Chicken Breasts with Asparagus-and-Rice Stuffing

"Asparagus is a delicate fruite, and wholesome for everiebodie, and especially when it is thickke, tender and sweete, and no very much boiled, it giveth good stomach unto the sicke . . . and makketh a good colour in the face. . ." —ANONYMOUS, *ca. 1600*

If you wish, serve with braised carrots and dill.

PREPARATION TIME *20 minutes*
COOKING *50 minutes*

4 whole boned chicken breasts, with skin, halved
1 clove garlic, peeled and crushed
1 pound medium-size asparagus stalks
2¼ cups liquid, part from cooking the asparagus, and part chicken stock
1 cup long-grain rice
½ teaspoon white pepper
½ teaspoon grated lemon zest
1 tablespoon grated Parmesan
Salt to taste
1 tablespoon oil
¼ cup wheat germ or unseasoned bread crumbs
Sprigs of lemon verbena for garnish

1. Preheat the oven to 350°F.

2. Place chicken fillets between 2 sheets of wax paper, pound them flat, and rub both sides with garlic.

3. Cut off woody part of the bottoms of the asparagus stalks. Arrange them in a bunch, tie together with twine, and steam in boiling water for 15 to 20 minutes, or until the stalks are tender yet crisp. Remove asparagus, rinse under cold water, and cut into small pieces.

4. Combine cooking liquid with stock to obtain 2¼ cups, and bring to a boil in a medium-size pot. Add rice, reduce the heat, cover tightly, and cook for 20 minutes. Check for doneness; if necessary, add more liquid, and stir up the rice grains with a fork.

5. Add pepper and grated lemon zest, fold in the asparagus, stir in the grated Parmesan, and adjust seasoning. Place 2 to 3 tablespoons in the center of each fillet. Flatten out slightly and fold side pieces over to form a neat package. Brush the outsides with oil, sprinkle lightly with wheat germ or bread crumbs, and secure with 2 toothpicks.

6. Place in the preheated oven, fastened side up, and bake for 8 to 10 minutes. Place remaining stuffing in a casserole dish, add ¼ cup stock if needed, and cover. Bake along with the chicken for 15 to 20 minutes. Turn the chicken with tongs and bake an additional 8 to 10 minutes.

7. Remove the chicken, discard the toothpicks, and arrange over baked asparagus-and-rice stuffing. Decorate with sprigs of lemon verbena. *Serves 4.*

Roasted Free-Range Chicken with Fresh Morels

Whatever happened to spring chickens? At seven weeks, these birds usually went from the yard to the table without stopping at the supermarket. The closest we have today to a spring chicken is the "free-range" chicken—birds allowed to roam freely in the barnyard, helping themselves to food that is free of antibiotics, growth hormones, or stimulants. The meat of free-range chickens is usually dense, tender, and flavorful. It is also expensive, but the higher price is worth it for a special dinner. That's why I have chosen it for our spring menu.

Since we are celebrating spring, we may as well go all out and treat ourselves to fresh morels, the first wild mushrooms to appear in the spring. Their nutty, bosky flavor is unique. They only grow in certain areas of the United States and Europe, and are difficult to locate and costly to buy. Dried morels can be substituted if fresh morels are unobtainable.

A simple green salad with a lemon vinaigrette dressing makes a refreshing accompaniment to this dish.

PREPARATION TIME *20 minutes*
COOKING *1 hour and 15 minutes*

One 3½-pound free-range chicken
Juice of ½ lemon
2 bay leaves, coarsely cut
6 juniper berries
4 black peppercorns
1 tablespoon butter
2 tablespoons minced shallots
12 large fresh morel caps, wiped clean and trimmed, or 1½ ounces dried morels (see hint)
Salt and freshly ground black pepper to taste
¼ cup Madeira
½ cup chicken stock
Finely chopped fresh dill

1. Preheat the oven to 425°F.

2. Sprinkle the cavity of the chicken with lemon juice. Tie the bay leaves, juniper berries, and peppercorns in cheesecloth, and put them in the chicken cavity. Truss the chicken as directed on page 6.

3. Put the chicken, breast up, in a shallow roasting pan, and place in the middle of the preheated oven. Let it brown for 15 minutes.

4. While it is browning, heat 1 tablespoon butter in a skillet, add shallots, and sauté for 2 minutes. Add morels, sauté for another 2 minutes, season with salt and pepper, and set aside.

5. Turn the chicken and let it brown on the other side for 15 minutes. Reduce heat to 375°F., and arrange the shallot-and-morel mixture around the chicken. Baste every 15 minutes with rendered juices. Roast for another 30 to 35 minutes.

6. Test for doneness before removing the chicken from the oven. When it is fully cooked, remove the trussing string and seasonings, remove it from the pan and let it rest for 10 minutes.

7. Place the roasting pan on top of the stove over medium heat. Skim off the fat. Add the Madeira and chicken stock, and bring to a rapid boil, scraping up coagulated juices with a wooden spoon. Remove from the heat, add the dill, and adjust seasoning.

8. Place the chicken on a serving platter and arrange shallots and morels around it. *Serves 4.*

Hint

If you use dried morels, put them in a small saucepan with 3 cups of water and bring to a boil. Turn off the heat and let the mushrooms steep for 30 minutes. Drain and rinse under cold running water to remove all the dirt. Pat dry and proceed with the recipe.

Chicken Fillets with Rhubarb Sauté

Although rhubarb is regarded as a fruit, it is really a vegetable. Introduced to Europe by way of the Volga region, it has long been valued for its alleged purgative and astringent qualities, as well as its fresh, tart taste. This dish goes very nicely with steamed rice and a platter of raw sugar snap peas and baby carrots.

PREPARATION TIME *10 minutes*
COOKING *15 minutes*

4 whole boneless and skinless chicken breasts
Flour to dust
White pepper
3 teaspoons oil
2 tablespoons butter
1 pound fresh rhubarb, thinly peeled, cut on the diagonal into 1-inch pieces
Juice of ½ lemon
1 teaspoon sugar
Salt to taste
Chopped parsley for garnish

1. Cut breasts in half to make 8 fillets, and flatten them with a mallet or rolling pin between 2 sheets of wax paper. Dry the fillets and dust them lightly with flour mixed with the pepper.

2. Heat the oil in a large skillet, add the chicken, and sauté for 3 minutes on one side. Add the butter and sauté for another 2 minutes, then turn and sauté for 3 to 4 minutes more. Remove the chicken and set it aside on a warm platter.

3. Add the rhubarb to the pan. Sauté over high heat for about 3 to 4 minutes, or until pieces are tender but still firm. Add the lemon juice and sugar, and stir. Taste for seasoning.

4. Slice the fillets into 1-inch strips. Arrange them, fanlike, on one side of a serving platter and place rhubarb on the outside of the dish. Sprinkle chicken with chopped parsley, and serve. *Serves 4.*

Baked Chicken with Fresh Herbs

Two signs unmistakably signal to me the arrival of spring: blooming forsythia in Central Park and the appearance of herbs in my country garden. Fresh herbs receive star billing in this dish—a regular on our restaurant's spring menu, and one of my husband's favorites. Serve it with homemade french fries and braised white onions.

PREPARATION TIME *10 minutes*
MARINATING *24 or more hours*
COOKING *35 minutes*

One 2½-pound chicken
1 tablespoon olive oil
Salt and pepper to taste

Marinade

½ cup olive oil
Juice of 1 lemon
4 shallots, peeled
4 cloves garlic, peeled
½ cup fresh dill
4 sprigs of rosemary
1 cup fresh basil
7 sprigs of thyme
½ cup tarragon leaves

1. Cut the chicken into the following pieces: 2 suprêmes, 2 drumsticks, and 2 thighs.
2. Put the marinade ingredients in a food processor and purée.
3. Let the chicken marinate in this mixture for at least 24 hours, turning pieces occasionally.
4. Preheat the oven to 475°F.
5. Remove the chicken from the marinade. Heat the oil in an ovenproof skillet. Brown the chicken, skin side first, for 5 minutes on each side. Place it in the preheated oven and bake for about 25 minutes, turning once. Season with salt and pepper. *Serves 4.*

Sautéed Fillets in Raspberry Vinegar Sauce

Fruit-flavored vinegars are very much in vogue these days. Actually, they were commonly used by the early settlers in this country, who found wild berries in such abundance that they happily incorporated them into many of their food preparations. In her book *Fancy Pantry,* Helen Witty gives instructions on how to make more than ten different kinds of flavored fruit and herb vinegars, including one for a richly flavored raspberry vinegar. Good commercial raspberry vinegar is readily available in specialty stores and some supermarkets.

Serve with that other summer winner, fresh sugar snap peas.

PREPARATION TIME *5 minutes*
COOKING *14 minutes*

2 whole boneless and skinless chicken breasts
Salt and freshly ground pepper to taste
3 tablespoons fresh tarragon leaves
½ cup raspberry vinegar
½ cup chicken stock
2 tablespoons Fromage Blanc (page 18)
1 cup fresh raspberries
Sprigs of parsley or mint for garnish

1. Cut the breasts in half to make 4 fillets. Dry the fillets and pound evenly between 2 sheets of wax paper. Season them with pepper and tarragon.

2. Dry-sauté the chicken in a hot nonstick pan for 3 minutes on each side. Combine the vinegar and chicken stock and add to the pan. Reduce heat, and let simmer for 8 minutes.

3. Remove the fillets, and arrange them on a serving platter.

4. Stir in fromage blanc, and heat through. Fold in the raspberries and adjust seasoning.

5. Spoon the sauce over the fillets, and garnish them with parsley or mint sprigs. *Serves 4.*

Baked Chicken with Red and Yellow Peppers

To complement the bright colors of the peppers in this dish, serve a cold salad of string beans with a shallot-flavored vinaigrette.

PREPARATION TIME *20 minutes*
COOKING *30 minutes*

One 3½-pound chicken, cut into 8 pieces, with skin removed
1 small yellow onion, peeled and sliced
1 clove garlic, minced
1 red pepper, cored, seeded, and cut into strips
1 yellow pepper, cored, seeded, and cut into strips
½ cup apple cider
½ cup chicken stock
Sprigs of fresh thyme, coarsely chopped
Sprigs of fresh marjoram, coarsely chopped
½ teaspoon salt
Chopped parsley for garnish

1. Preheat the oven to 375°F.

2. Sauté the chicken pieces in a nonstick pan for about 5 minutes on each side, set aside. Sauté the onion and garlic until slightly wilted, set aside. Sauté the peppers for about 2 minutes.

3. Add the stock, chicken pieces, onion, garlic, and peppers, and bring to a quick boil. Transfer everything to a large ovenproof dish, and sprinkle the thyme and marjoram over all.

4. Place in the preheated oven, and bake for about 20 minutes. Remove the chicken and vegetables, and arrange them on a serving platter.

5. Reduce the sauce by rapid boiling. Add the salt, and adjust seasoning. Spoon the sauce over the chicken and peppers. Sprinkle with parsley and serve. *Serves 4.*

Barbecued Garlic Chicken with Mint

Mint has been used for flavoring since antiquity. It appears in one of the earliest Roman recipes—added to a cold chicken dish. The Romans took it to Britain, where it soon became an important summer herb. In Middle Eastern cooking, mint is indispensable.

This dish is just as tasty broiled in your oven as on an outdoor grill. A serving suggestion: corn on the cob and a tomato salad.

PREPARATION TIME *10 minutes*
MARINATING *1 hour*
COOKING *25 to 30 minutes*

Juice of 2 lemons
Grated zest of ½ orange
6 cloves garlic, crushed
½ cup oil
Salt and freshly ground black pepper to taste
One 3-pound chicken, cut up
½ cup finely chopped fresh mint

1. Combine the lemon juice, orange zest, garlic, oil, salt, and pepper. Pour over the chicken, and marinate for at least 1 hour.
2. Preheat a charcoal grill.
3. Remove the chicken from the marinade and grill for approximately 25 to 30 minutes, turning the chicken several times to prevent burning.
4. Reheat the remaining marinade to the boiling point; boil for a few minutes. Pour marinade over the chicken pieces and sprinkle with chopped mint. *Serves 4.*

Grilled Chicken de Laune

To eat or not to eat the daisies? The practice of cooking with flowers is ancient. At one time or another, day lilies, elderflowers, violets, yucca, carnations, squash blossoms, marigolds, and nasturtiums have found their way into the cook pot. Nasturtiums and other edible flowers are available in certain specialty shops during the warmer months.

Jonathan Waxman, a well-known New York chef and restaurant owner, supplied this recipe.

PREPARATION TIME *20 minutes*
COOKING *45 minutes*

One 3½- to 4-pound free-range chicken, cut into 8 pieces
3 pinches of salt
6 turns of a pepper grinder
1 cup olive oil
1 mango, peeled, seeded, and cut into cubes
1 papaya, peeled, seeded, and cut into cubes
Juice of 1 lime
1 cup cilantro leaves (Chinese parsley), finely chopped
18 nasturtium blossoms
¼ cup butter
1 bunch fresh mustard greens

1. Preheat the broiler.

2. Sprinkle the chicken pieces with salt and pepper. Grill or broil them until nicely cooked and golden brown. Set aside and keep warm.

3. Mix the olive oil, mango, papaya, lime juice, and cilantro, and set aside. Put 10 nasturtium blossoms along with the butter into a food processor, purée, and let stand for 3 minutes.

4. Gently heat the nasturtium butter, add the mustard greens, and cook for 2 minutes.

5. Spoon the mango mixture on 4 plates, and place chicken pieces on top. Garnish with cooked mustard greens and put 1 or 2 nasturtiums on each plate as decoration. *Serves 4.*

Fall

Chicken Hunter-Style

Traditionally, fall is the hunting season. What we are hunting here are wild mushrooms—not in the forest or countryside, but at the marketplace, where greater and greater varieties are appearing each year. These exotic mushrooms earn their keep by being infinitely more flavorful and subtle than their common and timid cousin. Boletes (the French cèpe or the Italian porcino) are meaty mushrooms with a rusty brown bun sitting squarely on a fat white stalk. To prepare, wipe them clean with a damp cloth, scrape out the mushy pores with a spoon, trim the base of the stems, and use.

Serve with boiled potatoes and a spinach-and-walnut salad.

PREPARATION TIME *35 minutes*
COOKING *1 hour and 45 minutes*

One 4-pound chicken, cut into serving pieces
¼ teaspoon crushed black peppercorns
2 tablespoons oil
3 tablespoons butter
½ pound small white onions, peeled
1 pound boletes, cleaned and cut into quarters
¼ cup cognac
Grated zest of ½ orange
1 teaspoon dried thyme
1½ cups chicken stock
1 tablespoon tomato paste
½ pound cremini mushrooms, cleaned and cut into strips
Salt and freshly ground pepper to taste
Chopped parsley for garnish

1. Preheat the oven to 325°F.

2. Dry the chicken pieces and rub crushed peppercorns into the skin.

3. Heat 1 tablespoon oil and 1 tablespoon butter in a large ovenproof skillet. Add the onions and brown, raise the heat, then add the boletes to brown. Remove the onions and mushrooms and set aside.

4. Add the remaining oil and butter, and brown the chicken pieces for about 4 minutes on each side.

5. Add the cognac, let it warm for a minute, then ignite. When flame has subsided, sprinkle on the orange zest and thyme.

6. Return the onions and half of the boletes to the skillet. Pour on 1 cup of stock and the tomato paste. Bring to a boil, reduce heat, cover, and place in the preheated oven.

7. After 30 minutes, add the other half of the boletes and more stock as needed. Bake for about another hour, or until chicken is very tender. Meanwhile, sauté the creminis in a bit of butter until crisp, season with salt and freshly ground pepper, and set aside.

8. Remove the chicken, keeping it on a warm plate. Heat sauce on top of the stove to reduce, skim off fat, and adjust seasoning. Return the chicken to casserole, top with cremini mushrooms. Sprinkle with parsley and serve directly from the casserole. *Serves 4.*

Baked Pumpkin Stuffed with Bulgur and Chicken

Bulgur, a precooked cracked wheat, is a staple in Middle Eastern cooking, where it is most frequently combined with chicken or lamb. Loose or packaged bulgur is available here in most health food stores and some supermarkets. Serve this harvest fare with sautéed broccoli and cranberry sauce.

PREPARATION TIME *25 minutes*
COOKING *2 hours*

1 medium-size pumpkin
2 teaspoons butter
1 pound boneless and skinless chicken, cut into small cubes
1 onion, chopped
2 celery ribs, chopped
¼ cup dried currants
Grated zest of ½ lemon
¼ teaspoon ground cinnamon
½ teaspoon freshly grated nutmeg
1 cup apple cider
½ cup bulgur, soaked in water for 20 minutes and drained
Salt and pepper to taste
2 tablespoons bread crumbs
Autumn leaves for garnish

1. Preheat the oven to 350°F.

2. Cut the top off the pumpkin, making the cut about 1 inch from the stem all around. Reserve the top for a lid. Remove the seeds and pulp from the pumpkin with a large spoon and reserve 2 cups of pulp, diced into cubes.

3. Heat the butter in a large skillet and brown the chicken cubes on all sides, about 4 minutes or so. Remove and set aside.

4. Sauté the onions and celery until slightly browned, about 3 minutes. Add the pumpkin pulp, currants, lemon zest, and spices, and mix well. Mix in the chicken. Pour the cider into the skillet, bring to a boil, cover, lower heat, and let simmer for 20 minutes.

5. Remove skillet from the heat, add bulgur, and salt and pepper to taste.*

6. Sprinkle the bread crumbs into the pumpkin bottom to coat, spoon the chicken mixture into the pumpkin, and cover with the top. Set on a baking sheet and bake in the preheated oven for about 1½ hours, or until the pumpkin is tender. Remove the pumpkin and serve it on a large platter, surrounded by autumn leaves. *Serves 4.*

*May be made ahead of time to this point and kept, covered, in refrigerator until ready to use.

Chicken Stew with Coriander Sauce

Coriander is one of the most ancient of herbs. It grew in the Hanging Gardens of Babylon and has been found in ancient Egyptian tombs. The children of Israel, on their long trek to the Promised Land, were nourished by manna " . . . which was as coriander." Fresh, green coriander is sold widely at Chinese markets. Looking very much like parsley, it has a tangy, bitter taste that blends happily with the nuts and dried prunes used in this recipe.

PREPARATION TIME *15 minutes*
COOKING *45 minutes*

One 3½-pound chicken, cut into serving pieces, with skin removed
Freshly ground pepper to taste
2 tablespoons oil
1 large onion, peeled and chopped
1 clove garlic, peeled and minced
1 cup canned tomatoes, drained and chopped
1 tablespoon gin
1 cup chicken stock
Salt to taste

Coriander Sauce

2 cups fresh coriander leaves
¼ cup chopped green onions
½ cup extra-virgin olive oil
2 tablespoons tarragon vinegar
½ cup shelled pecans or walnuts
6 prunes, pitted
¼ cup chopped fresh basil (optional)
2 tablespoons chopped fresh parsley
Salt to taste

1. To make the coriander sauce, combine all ingredients in a blender or food processor and blend well.
2. Wipe the chicken, season with pepper, and set aside.
3. Heat the oil in a heavy skillet, add the onions, and sauté until wilted. Add the garlic and cook briefly, then add the canned tomatoes. Cook over slow heat for 10 minutes.
4. Add the chicken pieces, spoon some of the sauce over them, cover, and cook for 10 minutes. Pour on gin and let it heat through.

Add stock and salt to taste, cover again, and continue cooking for 20 minutes.* Just before serving, remove from heat and stir in the coriander sauce. *Serves 4.*

*This dish may be done ahead to this point and reheated.

Hint

The coriander sauce may be made ahead of time and stored, in a tightly covered jar, in the refrigerator. It will keep up to 1 week.

Roasted Chicken Véronique

This is one of my favorite chicken dishes because it incorporates all the elements I like in a meal: It is easy to prepare, looks lovely, and has a fresh, piquant flavor due to the combination of lemon zest, grapes, and the chicken's own juices. Although *à la Véronique* is a classic French garnish using white grapes, I prefer to use seedless red grapes because they add more color to the dish.

Baked squash and stir-fried Swiss chard are pleasant accompaniments.

PREPARATION TIME *20 minutes*
COOKING *1 hour and 10 minutes*

Two 2-pound chickens
Salt and white pepper to taste
Grated zest of 4 lemons
2 tablespoons oil
2 tablespoons lemon juice
1 pound red seedless grapes
1 to 2 tablespoons Madeira
2 teaspoons butter

1. Preheat the oven to 425°F.
2. Wipe the chickens dry. Salt and pepper the inside of the birds and sprinkle with lemon zest. Mix together the oil and lemon juice. Rub the outside of the chicken with this mixture.
3. Wash the grapes, remove the stems, and fill the cavity of the chicken with the grapes.
4. Truss birds as directed on page 6. Place in a large, shallow ovenproof casserole just big enough to hold the birds, and roast in the preheated oven for 20 minutes to brown.
5. Reduce heat to 350°F., and baste with the rendered liquid. After 25 minutes, turn the birds carefully, baste with pan juices, and roast another 20 to 25 minutes. Remove from the oven and let rest for 10 minutes.
6. Meanwhile, skim fat from the pan juices, add the Madeira, whisk in the butter, and adjust seasonings. Remove the strings and carve each bird in half. Arrange on a serving platter, with each half holding grapes. Pour pan juices over all and serve. *Serves 4.*

Baked Chicken in Snow

Because the salt seals in the juices, chickens covered in salt and cooked are particularly succulent and moist. (The salt does not penetrate the meat.) Present the dish at the table in all its white, glistening glory before removing the salt crust. Delicious with braised kale and potato pancakes.

PREPARATION TIME *18 minutes*
COOKING *1 hour*

4 cups coarse salt (preferably kosher)
Two 2½-pound chickens
1½ teaspoon dried thyme
Dash of freshly grated nutmeg
Freshly ground black pepper
8 prunes, pitted
4 crab apples
1 cup cold water

1. Preheat the oven to 450°F.

2. Line one large roasting pan with aluminum foil and cover the foil with a thick layer of salt.

3. Sprinkle the chicken cavities with thyme, freshly grated nutmeg, and ground black pepper, and stuff with prunes and apples. Truss chickens according to directions on page 6.

4. Place both birds on top of the salt layer and cover completely with rest of the salt. Sprinkle with water to seal, and place in the preheated oven. Bake, uncovered, for about 1 hour.

5. Remove chickens and let them rest for 10 minutes. Present them at the table for all to see, then break the crust and remove all traces of the salt. If necessary, brush with warm water. Cut into halves and serve surrounded by fruit stuffing. *Serves 4.*

Roast Capon with Cranberry, Wild Mushroom, and Barley Stuffing

A capon falls somewhere between a turkey and a chicken in size, usually weighing from 7 to 10 pounds. Actually a castrated rooster, capons were originally developed by the Romans, who transformed many of their noisy birds into eunuchs of the barnyard. Losing their spurs and growing plump, the capons were prized for their tender meat. Today, roosters are simply injected with hormones to achieve the same result. However, some of the farmers who raise their poultry in the free-range style have gone back to the old method, preferring their capons to grow slowly, without the use of chemical additives.

This particular capon dish is an ideal Thanksgiving or Christmas feast. I strongly suggest that you prepare the barley stuffing well ahead of time, since the raw barley must be soaked for at least 1 hour. The stuffing keeps well in a covered container in the refrigerator. Steamed cauliflower is an ideal companion to this dish.

PREPARATION TIME *2 hours*
COOKING *6 hours*

Stuffing

¾ cup raw barley
1 tablespoon butter
8 ounces fresh shiitake or cremini mushrooms, sliced
1 large onion, chopped
Freshly ground pepper to taste
2½ cups boiling water or chicken stock
1 cup buttermilk
1 cup fresh cranberries
Grated zest of 1 orange
½ cup cold water

Capon

One 8-pound capon
4 garlic cloves
1 tablespoon paprika, preferably sweet Hungarian
1 small onion, studded with 1 clove
2 tablespoons oil
Salt to taste
Sprigs of parsley for garnish
Kumquats (optional)

1. To cook barley: Cover the barley with cold water in a small saucepan, and bring to a boil. Remove from the heat, cover, and allow to stand for 1 hour.

2. Preheat the oven to 350°F.

3. Heat the butter in a large skillet, stir in the mushrooms and onion, and sauté for 5 minutes. Sprinkle with pepper.

4. Add the cooked barley and cook over moderate heat, stirring constantly, until barley is lightly toasted, about 5 minutes. Transfer barley mixture to a large ungreased casserole.

5. Add the boiling water or stock to mixture, stir, then fold in the buttermilk. Adjust seasoning. Cover and bake in the preheated oven until barley mixture is tender, about 1¼ hours.

6. Meanwhile, wash the cranberries. Place them in an enamel pot with the orange zest, add the cold water, and bring to a boil. Reduce heat and let simmer until barely cooked, about 10 minutes. Strain off excess liquid and set aside until ready to use.

7. Carefully fold the cranberries into the barley mixture. Add some additional liquid, if necessary. Cool.

8. Preheat oven to 450°F.

9. Dry the inside of the capon with paper towels. Rub the cavity with garlic, sprinkle with paprika, and place clove-studded onion in the body cavity. Loosely fill cavity with barley stuffing. (Any remaining stuffing can be baked in oven with capon for the last 1¼ hours of cooking time.) Close the opening with skewers and truss as directed on page 6. Rub the outside of the bird with oil and salt.

10. Set stuffed capon on rack in a large roasting pan and put in the preheated oven. After 20 minutes, reduce the heat to 350°F., basting capon with pan drippings.

11. Remove the bird from oven when done, in about 2½ to 3 hours. Check to see if drumsticks move freely and juices run clear. Let the capon rest for 20 minutes. Transfer stuffing to a separate serving bowl. Discard onion. Surround capon with sprigs of parsley and kumquats. *Serves 4.*

Hint

When cooking a large, freshly killed bird, it is advisable to let it sit in the refrigerator for a few days. This allows the meat to relax and become more tender.

Pot au Feu

Few dishes in winter are as comforting and as stomach warming as soup. And few soups are as satisfying as *pot au feu,* or "a pot on the fire." A quintessential French dish, pot au feu is made with whatever meat or vegetable is available on a particular day. Some families keep it going for days, replenishing the pot with a veal shank one day, and a head of cabbage another. The preparation and chopping are part of the fun, especially when you can get family members and friends to help you. I suggest you cook the chicken in the broth the night before, both for ease of preparation and for a more savory broth.

PREPARATION TIME *1 hour*
COOKING *overnight plus 2½ hours*

One 5-pound chicken, cut into 8 pieces
1 large bouquet garni composed of 3 bay leaves, 4 parsley stalks, 6 black peppercorns, 1 teaspoon dried thyme and 1 teaspoon dried rosemary tied in cheesecloth
1 medium onion, studded with 4 to 5 cloves
1 quart liquid (preferably half water, half chicken stock)
1 pound carrots, peeled
1 pound turnips, peeled
1 celery rib, trimmed
4 leeks, washed
Salt and pepper to taste
1 pound potatoes, peeled, left whole if small, otherwise halved or quartered
Chopped parsley for garnish

1. Trim the chicken pieces of excess fat.

2. Place the chicken in a large soup kettle, cover with cold water, cover, and bring to a boil. Remove chicken, rinse under cold water, and trim pieces again. Rinse the kettle.

3. Return the chicken to the kettle, add bouquet garni and studded onion, and pour on water and chicken stock. Bring to a quick boil, reduce heat, and let simmer for 1½ hours, skimming off any scum that may rise to the surface. Let cool and refrigerate overnight. When ready to proceed with recipe, remove all surface fat from chicken and broth.

4. Cut the carrots and turnips to about 2 inches in length, then slice them in strips (similar to thin french fries). Cut the celery and leeks to the same length, but slice them in wider strips.

5. Reheat chicken and broth, bring to a boil, and add celery and salt and pepper to taste. Cover, and continue to simmer for 15 minutes. At this point, cook the potatoes separately, starting in cold, slightly salted water, for about 25 to 30 minutes. Add the leeks to the pot, cook for another 15 minutes, then add the carrots and turnips. Cover, and continue cooking for 15 minutes.

6. When the chicken is well cooked (approximately 45 minutes to 1 hour), remove chicken pieces and place on a large, heated serving platter. Remove vegetables with a slotted spoon and arrange around the chicken. Drain the potatoes and add to the dish. Sprinkle generously with chopped parsley.

7. Discard bouquet garni and the onion. Strain soup broth through a fine sieve, then pour into a heated soup tureen or deep serving dish. Bring everything to the table and serve chicken and vegetables in individual soup plates and pour some of the broth over. *Serves 4.*

Hint

Leeks are extremely sandy. Make sure to wash and rinse them thoroughly. Most of the vegetables in this dish can be sliced ahead of time and kept in cold water until it's time to start the pot boiling.

Stuffed Cabbage

I grew up with cabbage. It appeared in many of our dishes, especially during the final long winter months when many of the vegetables stocked in our cellar had dwindled down to a bare minimum. Of all the cabbage dishes, stuffed cabbage was my favorite. Serve it with broad noodles and small green peas.

PREPARATION TIME *30 minutes*
COOKING *1 hour and 30 minutes*

1 large Savoy cabbage, about 1½ pounds
½ pound boneless and skinless raw chicken meat, cut into chunks (about 1 cup)
2 tablespoons oil
1 medium onion, chopped
2 eggs, lightly beaten
Grated zest of 1 lemon
½ teaspoon cinnamon
1 teaspoon paprika
½ teaspoon ground allspice
½ teaspoon salt
Pepper to taste
2 cups cooked rice
1 tablespoon butter
2 tart apples, peeled, cored, and chopped
½ cup chicken stock
1 cup canned tomatoes, drained
½ teaspoon sugar
1 tablespoon cider vinegar
6 juniper berries and 4 cloves, tied in cheesecloth

1. Blanch the cabbage in rapidly boiling salted water for 5 minutes. Take the cabbage out of the water, remove outer leaves carefully (for either 12 or 16 roulades), chop up the rest, and set aside. Remove about 1½ inches of the hard part of the bottom of the cabbage leaves.

2. Blend or chop chicken (raw meat chops easier when partially frozen), and set aside in a bowl. Heat 1 tablespoon oil in a large skillet, sauté the onion until lightly wilted. Add the onion to the chicken, together with eggs and seasonings. Mix well and fold in the rice.

3. Place 2 teaspoons of the chicken mixture in the center of each cabbage leaf. Fold 3 sides of the leaves toward the center, then roll.*

4. Heat the butter and remaining oil in the skillet and brown the roulades on both sides, about 10 minutes. Remove and set aside.

5. Raise the heat, toss in the chopped cabbage and apples, and sauté to brown slightly. Combine stock, tomatoes, sugar, and cider vinegar, and stir into cabbage-and-apple mixture.

6. Place the roulades on top of the mixture. Tuck cheesecloth bundle into one corner of skillet, cover, and simmer for 45 minutes. Remove the spice bundle and serve. *Serves 4.*

*This dish may be prepared ahead to this point. It can also be frozen for use at a later date.

8

Cooking for One

LUCULLUS is remembered as the greatest epicure of all time. An immensely wealthy Roman general, he lived lavishly. His table was graced with the rarest of foods, and his banquets were legendary—the costs defied imagination. Dining alone one evening, he startled his servants by demanding even greater delicacies, ending up with a dazzling array of superb dishes. The occasion, he explained grandly, was a special one, for "tonight, Lucullus dines with Lucullus."

Some evenings I may dine as Lucullus; other evenings I am more casual. I may even put my meal on a tray and eat wherever I feel most comfortable. These recipes reflect both kinds of dining styles.

Paillard with White, Black, and Green Peppercorns

The secret of this light and quick dish lies in the quality of the ingredients: extra-virgin olive oil and peppercorns crushed on the spot (see hint on page 92), which render them more flavorful and less bitter. Serve with an arugula salad.

PREPARATION TIME *8 minutes*
COOKING *1½ minutes*

1 whole boneless and skinless chicken breast, halved
½ teaspoon white peppercorns, crushed
½ teaspoon black peppercorns, crushed
½ teaspoon green peppercorns, crushed
1 tablespoon extra-virgin olive oil
Juice of ¼ lemon
Chopped parsley for garnish

1. Trim each fillet and slip between 2 pieces of wax paper. Pound very thin on both sides with a mallet or rolling pin.
2. Rub the crushed peppercorns into both sides of the fillets. Put oil on a plate and coat fillets.
3. Heat an iron skillet to very, very hot. Remove fillets from plate and let oil drip off them completely. Place them in the hot skillet, and sear 45 seconds on each side. Squeeze lemon over them, add a bit of oil, and sprinkle with parsley. *Serves 1.*

Roast Squab

As a child I thrived on both food and fairy stories. I particularly liked the story about never-never land: Three children, tired from working in the fields, are each granted a wish. "I wish we were in never-never land, never having to work again," said one. Instantly the wish comes true. Leading an idle life, they are soon too lazy to bother preparing their own food. Resting under a tree, they grow more and more hungry. "I wish that a roasted squab would come flying straight into our mouths," says the second child, whereupon three roasted squabs come zooming through the air, complete with knives, forks, and napkins! Their third wish returned them home, happy and sated.

Excellent with braised brussels sprouts.

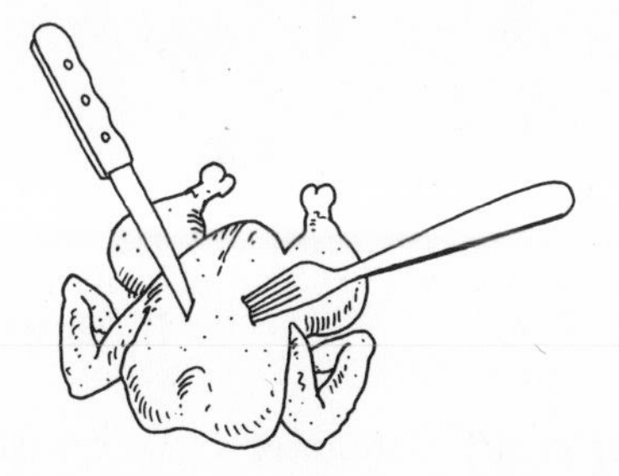

PREPARATION TIME *8 minutes*
COOKING *35 minutes*

1 squab
1 teaspoon fresh lemon juice
1 teaspoon dried tarragon
White pepper and salt to taste
2 tablespoons olive oil

1. Preheat oven to 400°F.

2. Wipe the squab inside and out. Rub the cavity with lemon juice and sprinkle with tarragon, salt, and pepper. Brush the surface of the bird with oil and truss as directed on page 6.

3. Arrange the squab breast side down in a shallow roasting pan. Roast for 20 minutes. Turn breast side up and roast for another 15 minutes. Test the leg for doneness, or puncture the joints to check if juices run clear.

4. Transfer the squab to a platter and let rest for 10 minutes. Discard string. *Serves 1.*

Steamed Chicken Basket with Aïoli

This is a particularly wholesome dish, easy to make and ready in no time. If prepared ahead, place food in steamer basket, cover with plastic wrap, and refrigerate.

PREPARATION TIME *12 minutes*
COOKING *8 minutes*

½ head of lettuce
1 whole boneless and skinless chicken breast
1 small zucchini, cut into strips
1 tomato, quartered
1 carrot, peeled and sliced on the diagonal, or any combination of red pepper, cored and cut into strips; broccoli or cauliflower florets; or fennel, quartered
Oil
½ teaspoon dried thyme

Aïoli

½ cup light mayonnaise (see page 15)
1 clove garlic, peeled and crushed
1½ teaspoons lemon juice

1. Line the bottom of a steamer basket with lettuce leaves. Divide chicken breast into 2 fillets, and flatten between 2 sheets of wax paper with a mallet or rolling pin.

2. Arrange vegetables and fillets over leaves. Brush lightly with oil and sprinkle with thyme.

3. Place over a pot of rapidly boiling water. Cover, and steam for 8 minutes. Set steamer on a plate and serve with aïoli. (To make aïoli, beat the garlic and lemon juice into the mayonnaise.) *Serves 1.*

Sautéed Suprêmes with Yellow Pepper and Watercress

I'm a great admirer of balsamic vinegar, a complex condiment that was highly esteemed some 900 years ago. It was thought to have curative powers, hence its name. Even today, some people value it as a digestive.

PREPARATION TIME *10 minutes*
COOKING *16 minutes*

1 or 2 suprêmes, skin removed
White pepper to taste
2 teaspoons extra-virgin olive oil
1 yellow pepper, cored and thinly sliced
1 tablespoon plain wheat germ
1 small clove garlic, minced
2 tablespoons orange juice
1 tablespoon balsamic vinegar
1 bunch watercress, stems removed and chopped, about 1 cup
Black pepper to taste

1. Season the suprêmes with white pepper. Heat 1 teaspoon of oil in a skillet and sauté suprêmes 3 to 4 minutes on each side. Remove to a warm platter, and cover.

2. Add the remaining oil and sauté the pepper for 5 minutes. Add wheat germ and garlic, and sauté until slightly browned.

3. Add orange juice and vinegar, and heat through for about 1 minute. Mix in the watercress, let it wilt, and remove pan from heat. Add black pepper to taste, adjust seasoning, and arrange vegetables over the chicken. *Serves 1.*

Sautéed Suprême with Chanterelles

I grew up with chanterelle mushrooms, called *Pfifferling* in Germany. I was intrigued by their funny shape—an upside-down umbrella with wrinkles—their sharp, peppery flavor, and their color, which ranged from pale yellow to deep orange. Today, I like nothing better than a heaping dish of sautéed chanterelles, although I will happily settle for a juicy suprême, all but smothered by my favorite fungi. Enjoy it with fresh pasta and an escarole salad.

PREPARATION TIME *15 minutes*
COOKING *25 minutes*

1 suprême (page 10)
1 teaspoon oil
1 teaspoon butter
1 shallot, peeled and finely chopped
¼ pound chanterelles, cleaned, base of stem removed, and halved if too big
Salt and pepper to taste
1 teaspoon chopped fresh dill
Watercress for garnish

1. Dry the suprême. Heat the oil and butter in a skillet. Add shallot and sauté for 2 minutes. Toss in chanterelles and sauté over high heat for 5 minutes. Remove shallot and mushrooms, and set aside.

2. Sauté suprême, skin side down, for 7 to 8 minutes. Turn, and sauté for another 7 to 8 minutes. Put on a serving platter.

3. Return the shallot and mushrooms to the skillet for 1 minute to heat through. Season to taste with salt and pepper, and arrange over the suprême. Sprinkle with chopped dill and garnish with watercress. *Serves 1.*

Hint

There is considerable controversy about whether or not to wash wild mushrooms. Those in favor of washing hold that it in no way impairs the flavor; those against argue that it weakens the flavor in addition to bloating the mushrooms. The best way to get rid of sand and grit is to tap each mushroom lightly to loosen the dirt, and then to wipe the stem and cap with a soft, damp cloth. In extreme cases I have cleaned mushrooms with a toothbrush. If that doesn't help, wash them quickly under cold running water and dry immediately.

Chicken Nuggets with Cabbage

This quickly prepared dish supplies necessary protein, vitamins, and minerals. A side dish of cold sesame noodles will do the rest.

PREPARATION TIME *15 minutes*
COOKING *12 minutes*

1 cup white wine
Juice of 1 lemon
2 shallots, finely chopped
2 cups shredded, paper-thin cabbage
½ boneless and skinless chicken breast, cut into bite-size nuggets
2 teaspoons flour
1 teaspoon oil
1 teaspoon butter
Salt and pepper to taste
Chopped parsley for garnish

1. Heat the wine and lemon juice in a saucepan. Add the shallots and cabbage, and steam for 2 minutes. Remove the cabbage and set aside. Continue simmering the liquid to reduce, then return cabbage and season with pepper.

2. Dust the chicken lightly with flour. Heat the oil and butter in a skillet. Toss in the chicken nuggets and sauté for 5 minutes. Adjust seasoning.

3. Arrange a cabbage ring on a serving platter. Place the chicken over it and pour shallots and sauce over chicken. Sprinkle with chopped parsley. *Serves 1.*

Chicken Breast with Fresh Rosemary Broiled over Bread

This dish is simplicity itself, and so good I could eat it twice a week. The bread, which soaks up the accumulated drippings, is the best part. Try this dish with chick-pea salad.

PREPARATION TIME *6 minutes*
COOKING *18 minutes*

½ boneless chicken breast, with skin left on
1 teaspoon oil
1 teaspoon lemon juice
2 sprigs fresh rosemary, chopped, or ½ teaspoon dried
2 slices bread
Freshly ground pepper

1. Preheat the broiler.
2. Trim the chicken breast.
3. Line a broiler pan with aluminum foil. Put the bread on the foil and place the chicken breast on the bread. (Trim the bread to fit the chicken piece, so the bread doesn't burn.)
4. Brush the underside of the chicken breast with oil, then dab with some of the lemon juice, and sprinkle with half of the rosemary. Broil for 10 minutes.
5. Turn the chicken, skin side up, and brush with oil, lemon juice, and remaining rosemary. Broil for an additional 8 minutes. Remove, let cool slightly.
6. Transfer bread and chicken to a serving dish using a spatula. Add the freshly ground pepper. *Serves 1.*

Hint

Leftover fresh herbs will keep for over a week if preserved in coarse salt.

Ready-Cooked Chicken with Stir-fried Broccoli and Pine Nuts

Sometimes it just does not pay to start dinner from scratch. By the time you have bought and cooked the necessary items, you have spent more time and money than a little dinner calls for. Fortunately take-out chicken places have sprung up all over the country—a great convenience, as well as an opportunity to transform ordinary food into splendid fare by adding a few personal touches to it.

I suggest you try this dish with boiled rice and pickled beet salad.

PREPARATION TIME *10 minutes*
COOKING *15 minutes*

½ ready-cooked barbecued chicken (2 cups)
½ package frozen broccoli florets
2 teaspoons butter
¼ cup pine nuts
Salt and pepper to taste

1. Debone chicken and remove skin. Cut into medium-size chunks; set aside.

2. Parboil the broccoli until just crisp (do not overcook).

3. Melt the butter in a skillet or wok, and sauté broccoli over high heat for about 5 minutes. Add pine nuts and stir. Add chicken pieces to warm through. Season with salt and pepper. *Serves 1.*

Marinated and Baked Herb Chicken

Good with stir-fried snow peas and stuffed mushrooms.

PREPARATION TIME *10 minutes*
MARINATING *2 hours or more*
COOKING *20 minutes*

Marinade

⅓ cup tomato juice
Juice of ½ lemon
½ clove garlic, minced
¼ teaspoon dried oregano
¼ teaspoon dried basil
¼ teaspoon dried thyme

1 whole boneless and skinless chicken breast, cut into bite-size pieces

Salt and pepper to taste

1. Combine tomato and lemon juices, garlic, and herbs. Pour over the chicken, cover, and marinate in the refrigerator for at least 2 hours.

2. Preheat the oven to 350°F.

3. Place chicken in a shallow baking pan, and spread marinade evenly over it. Bake for about 20 minutes, turning once. Adjust seasoning. *Serves 1.*

Chicken Around the World

SOME people call it *ayam, aves, pollo, poulet, fango,* or *murgh*. We call it chicken, that most universal of foods. Chickens were first domesticated by the Chinese. The meat became a staple in Oriental cuisines, and then slowly made its way to Europe and eventually to the Americas. Whether poached, stir-fried, skewered on spits, baked in clay, pickled or pounded, stuffed with fruits, rubbed with mint, perfumed by cinnamon, cumin, coriander, or ginger, flavored by olives or garlic, or spiked with chili, chicken is the ultimate ambassador of all nations, as diversified as the world's many languages and customs.

How to Find Ingredients

Every city in the United States has specific ethnic neighborhoods, covering a few blocks or perhaps a good part of a town. A trip to these areas will not only help you find the item you want but will also put you in touch with the sights, smells, and sounds of other worlds.

Latin American communities dot the country. Their bodegas and supermercados are ideal places to shop for the basic ingredients of their exciting dishes. In addition, almost every American supermarket has a sizable section devoted to canned, dried, and ready-made Latin American products.

Oriental groceries and produce stores—particularly common on the East and West coasts—carry a substantial line of Chinese and Japanese products. Canned and bottled Oriental food items are also found in the special gourmet sections of most supermarkets.

Although nothing compares with an authentic Indian, Moroccan, or Middle Eastern store where spices are freshly ground to order, the most commonly used spices are packaged and displayed on the spice shelf in most specialty food stores and supermarkets. When purchasing a spice, buy the smallest size available, put the date of purchase on the label, and close the container tightly after each use. Once in a while, take stock of your spice cabinet, and throw out a spice or dried herb that you have not used in a long time.

Local health food stores often carry hard-to-find Oriental and Indian staples, as well as other ethnic foods. In addition, many mail-order houses specializing in herbs, spices, and regional items will send their catalogues on request. You can locate them by checking the source information in ethnic cookbooks, scanning the yellow pages, or checking the home section of your local newspaper.

I have indicated suitable substitutes for ingredients in these recipes whenever appropriate. If all else fails, as I've mentioned before, improvise. Many well-known dishes originated by accident.

MIDDLE EAST

Djaaj Biltoon

Garlic Chicken with Potato-and-Mint Purée

This Middle Eastern dish offers an exciting contrast between the sizzling, crisp chicken and the cold, smooth purée.

PREPARATION TIME *25 minutes*
MARINATING *4 hours or overnight*
COOKING *45 minutes*

Purée

¾ cup oil
1 clove garlic, peeled and crushed
3 tablespoons lime juice
3 medium potatoes, peeled and boiled
2 tablespoons fresh mint, or 1 teaspoon dried

4 cloves garlic, minced
½ cup oil
Juice of 2 lemons
4 whole chicken legs (drumsticks and thighs)
Thin slices of 1 lemon for garnish
Thin slices of 1 lime for garnish

To make purée:

1. Put half of the oil and the garlic in a blender, mix. Add lime juice and potatoes and blend.
2. Add the remaining oil and mint, and blend until smooth. Adjust seasoning, possibly adding more lime juice. Cover, and store in the refrigerator until ready to use.

To make chicken:

3. Combine garlic, oil, and lemon juice. Pour over the chicken pieces and let marinate for at least 4 hours or overnight.
4. Preheat broiler to 350°F. Place chicken pieces, skin side down, on broiler rack. Brush generously with marinade, and broil for 20 minutes. Turn, brush again, and broil for another 20 minutes. Test for doneness.
5. Place on a serving platter. Garnish with thin slices of lemon and lime, and serve hot with accompanying cold potato-and-mint purée. *Serves 4.*

SOUTH AFRICA

Ayam Panggang Pedis

Spicy Chicken

South African cuisine comes from the Dutch, who settled in the Bantu country some 300 years ago, and from the Malaysians, who were brought in as slaves to help develop the country. The spices they brought from East India heavily influenced the robust but fairly bland Dutch diet. In fact, it's often hard to tell some South African dishes from those of Indonesia.

Traditionally, this spicy dish is cooled down by any of these serving suggestions: baked bananas, sliced papaya with shredded coconut, or chopped cucumber with yogurt.

PREPARATION TIME *25 minutes*
COOKING *50 minutes*

Sauce

1 cup chicken stock
1½ cups tomato sauce
½ cup red wine vinegar
4 tablespoons frozen apple juice concentrate
2 teaspoons light (low-salt) soy sauce
Juice of 2 lemons
1 teaspoon sugar
4 cloves garlic, peeled and crushed
2 teaspoons powdered cumin
2 teaspoons powdered turmeric
1 teaspoon grated fresh gingerroot
½ teaspoon red pepper flakes
½ teaspoon dry mustard

One 4-pound chicken, cut into 8 pieces
1 teaspoon oil
1 large onion, chopped
Salt and white pepper to taste

1. Prepare the sauce by blending all sauce ingredients in blender or food processor. Set aside.

2. Dry the chicken pieces and season with pepper. Brush the bottom of a large skillet with oil to coat. When hot, add the chicken pieces and brown on both sides, about 5 minutes per side. Remove and set aside.

3. Quick-sauté the onion until translucent. Add sauce mixture to skillet, raise heat, and cook 15 to 20 minutes, stirring occasionally.

Return chicken to skillet, lower heat, and cook, covered, for another 20 minutes, or until chicken pieces are tender.

4. Arrange chicken on a large platter. Adjust seasoning, and spoon sauce over chicken. *Serves 4.*

Hint

In earlier days few South Africans owned a blender or food processor. They pounded or blended their spices in a mortar, as did their ancestors centuries ago. For a more authentic flavor, you might try this slower but time-honored method.

SENEGAL

Mafe

Groundnut Stew

Rice and millet, yam, sweet potatoes, cassava, banana, plantain, mango, and papaya are the staples of the West African diet. Chicken and goat are the common meats; soups and stews are the dishes served most often, usually thickened with okra. Tomato and chili peppers add flavor, while peanuts (called "groundnuts") supply more protein.

Mafe is a main dish commonly found in all of West Africa, including Togo, Nigeria, Ghana, and Senegal. It is a dish beloved by all, but about whose preparation no two families agree. Hawa Diallo, Senegal's officer of economic affairs at the United Nations, says she would be reluctant to eat the dish in anyone's house but hers, simply because the preparation of *mafe* is so much a matter of personal preference. I am grateful to her for her generous advice on the following recipe, which is traditionally served with sweet potatoes.

PREPARATION TIME *15 minutes*
COOKING *40 minutes*

½ cup peanut oil
One 3½-pound chicken, cut into small pieces
Salt and pepper to taste
1 large onion, chopped
½ cup tomato paste, diluted with ½ cup water
2 hot chilies, with seeds removed, crushed
2 tablespoons smooth peanut butter (without sugar)
2 to 3 tablespoons water
1 package frozen baby okra, cooked as directed on package
Chili powder to taste
3 cups cooked long-grain rice

1. Heat the oil in a large skillet with a lid. Brown the chicken pieces, remove, season with salt and pepper, and set aside.

2. Remove oil. Brown the onion until translucent. Add the thinned-out tomato paste to skillet, stir well. Add the chicken and chilies, cover, reduce heat, and let simmer for 20 minutes.

3. Warm the peanut butter in a small saucepan over medium heat, remove pan from heat, and add enough water to make a smooth paste. Stir this into the stew. (Use a wooden spoon—a metal one will break up the sauce.) Continue to simmer for 5 to 10 minutes, or until chicken is tender. (Add additional liquid only if necessary since the stew should be thick.)

4. Add the cooked okra to the stew. If you want a hotter version, add chili powder to taste. Place cooked rice in the center of a deep dish, and spoon the stew over it. *Serves 4.*

Hint

Okra, no matter how it's cooked, tends to be slippery and slimy—the very nature of this tender, sweet-tasting vegetable.

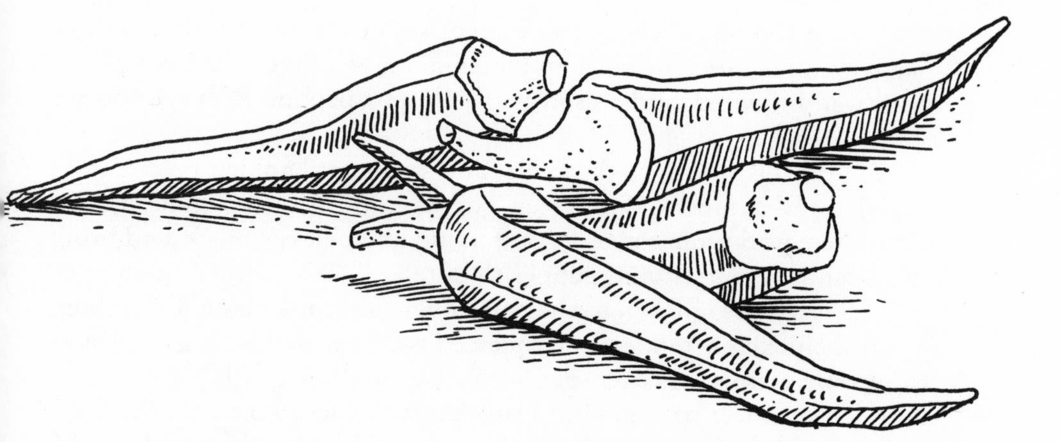

HUNGARY

Paprikás Csirke

Chicken Paprika

Paprika, which is as Hungarian as gypsy music, was originally grown in America. Once a very hot spice, it became more and more mellow as it grew in the great Hungarian plains until it assumed the mild and sweet flavor that distinguishes it today. Meant to color as well as flavor, it is one of the few spices that can be used by the spoonful. Good paprika should have a brilliant red color; if it looks brown, it is probably stale. This dish is usually served with spaetzle, and a salad of cucumber and dill.

PREPARATION TIME *30 minutes*
COOKING *1 hour*

3 tablespoons oil
Two 2½-pound broiling chickens, quartered
Salt and pepper to taste
2 medium onions, finely chopped
3 tablespoons sweet Hungarian paprika
2 cloves garlic, minced
½ pound mushrooms, cleaned and thickly sliced
2 green peppers, seeded and cut into 1-inch chunks
1 bay leaf
1 cup canned plum tomatoes, drained, liquid reserved
1 cup chicken stock
1 tablespoon flour
1 cup Fromage Blanc (page 18)
Chopped parsley for garnish

1. Heat the oil in a large stovetop casserole dish or a 12-inch frying pan with a lid. Add the chicken pieces, a few at a time. Sauté both sides until well-browned, and season with salt and pepper. Remove and set aside.

2. Add the onions to the skillet and sauté until golden brown. Add paprika, garlic, mushrooms, green peppers, and bay leaf, and sauté for 2 minutes. Add plum tomatoes and liquid and chicken stock, and bring to a simmer. Add salt and pepper to taste.

3. Return the chicken to the pan, cover, and cook about 45 minutes, or until chicken is tender when pierced with a fork. Using a large slotted spoon, transfer chicken pieces to a warm serving dish.

4. Discard the bay leaf and bring the sauce to a boil. Mix the flour with 1 ladleful of sauce, and add this to the Fromage Blanc and stir.

5. Slowly pour this mixture into the hot sauce, stirring until well blended. Adjust seasoning, and pour the sauce over the chicken. Garnish with chopped parsley and serve. *Serves 4.*

Hint

To further enhance the flavor of this dish, briefly remove the pan from the fire when you are adding the paprika, then proceed with the recipe.

CHINA

Jiang You Ji

Five-Spice Chicken

Chickens were first domesticated by the Chinese and have always been an important part of their diet. The Chinese will use one large chicken in several different ways, never wasting an ounce. The white meat is thinly sliced and reserved for such banquet dishes as velvet chicken. The dark meat is spiced, often in a peppery marinade, and usually steamed. Gizzards are stir-fried with lots of vegetables, and the carcass makes a delicious soup, particularly when cooked with Chinese black mushrooms.

I learned to cook the following dish in Florence Lin's Chinese cooking class, where we used a 6-pound chicken, split in half. (The other half was frozen for future use.) We prepared and served the dish along with jasmine rice and a hot lettuce salad.

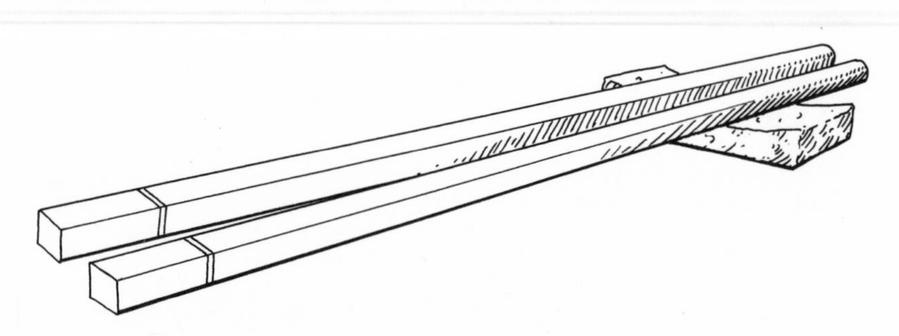

PREPARATION TIME *10 minutes*
COOKING *25 minutes*
COOLING *30 to 45 minutes*

One-half 6-pound chicken, or one 3½-pound chicken, split
1 teaspoon salt

Marinade

1 cup light (low-salt) soy sauce
½ cup Chinese rice wine or dry sherry
⅛ cup rock sugar candy, or 1 tablespoon light corn syrup
2 cups water

1 spice bundle, or 1 teaspoon of 5-Spice Powder, or wrap the following spices in a piece of cheesecloth:*
- *1 whole star anise*
- *1 piece cinnamon bark*
- *1-inch piece tangerine peel*
- *1 teaspoon fennel seeds*
- *5 Sichuan peppercorns*

1. Salt the chicken and set it aside for 15 minutes. Combine the marinade ingredients in a large, heavy skillet with a cover. Add the spice package and bring to a boil. Simmer for 10 minutes.

2. Rinse the salt off the chicken and place it, meaty side down, in the liquid. Bring again to a boil, reduce heat, cover, and simmer for 10 to 12 minutes. Turn the chicken skin side down and cook for another 15 minutes. Remove from the heat and let chicken cool in the liquid for 30 to 45 minutes.†

3. When cooled, remove chicken and chop with a cleaver into 1-by-2-inch pieces, and serve. *Serves 4.*

*This product, called Five-Spice for Spiced Food, can be purchased in Oriental grocery stores.

†This dish can be made ahead of time up to this point and refrigerated.

Hint

Strain any remaining marinade, remove any surface fat, and store for future use. It will keep in the refrigerator for 1 week or can be frozen. Be sure to boil for 2 or 3 minutes before reusing.

CENTRAL ASIA

Morgh-e Tu Por

Cornish Hen Stuffed with Bulgur, Apricots, and Sour Cherries

Central Asia traditionally covers the area from Afghanistan to Turkey, and includes Iran, Iraq, and the Soviet republics of Armenia, Georgia, and the Caucasus. It is a rugged region of mountains, steppes, and grasslands, with hot summers and cold winters. Barley and wheat dominate the diet; bulgur, a cracked wheat cereal, forms the basis for many dishes. Apples, apricots, pomegranates, plums, and almonds originated here, and cinnamon is the favorite spice. The following recipe is a composite of various Central Asian dishes. Using a Rock Cornish hen is my own invention.

PREPARATION TIME *30 minutes*
COOKING *55 minutes*

Stuffing

1 cup bulgur
3 tablespoons butter
2 medium onions, chopped, to make 1 cup
1¼ cups chicken stock
½ cup pitted dried sour cherries, or raisins
½ cup finely chopped dried apricots
½ teaspoon ground cinnamon
½ teaspoon ground allspice
Juice of 1 lemon
Grated zest of ½ lemon
Pinch of salt
Salt and pepper to taste

4 Rock Cornish hens, about 1¼ pounds each
2 tablespoons honey
4 tablespoons sesame seeds

1. To make stuffing, soak the bulgur in hot water to cover for 10 minutes, drain, squeeze out excess moisture, and set aside.

2. Heat 1 tablespoon butter, and sauté onions until translucent, about 5 minutes. Add bulgur, sauté, stirring constantly, until nutty brown, about 10 minutes. Add ½ cup stock, cherries or raisins, apricots, cinnamon, allspice, lemon juice, and lemon zest, and stir. Season with salt and pepper, cover, and set aside for 1 hour.*

3. Add more stock to stuffing, if necessary, reserving about ¼ cup for basting, and heat through, adjusting seasoning. Stuff each bird with equal parts of filling. Truss hens as directed on page 6.

4. Preheat the oven to 400°F.

5. Heat the remaining 2 tablespoons of butter in a pan, add the honey, and heat to bubbling. Roll birds, one at a time, in the honey mixture to coat them. Arrange them in a roasting pan, brush with remaining honey mixture, and place in the preheated oven.

6. Turn the birds after 20 minutes, basting with the remaining chicken stock. Roast for another 20 minutes, basting once. Turn them again, breast side up, sprinkle with sesame seeds, and roast for an additional 5 minutes, or until tender. Remove from the oven and let sit for 10 minutes before carving. *Serves 4.*

*The stuffing may be made ahead of time and stored, well covered, in the refrigerator.

CUBA

Arroz con Pollo

Rice with Chicken

Of all the islands in the Caribbean, Cuba is the most typically Spanish in background and cuisine. The major ingredients of this popular dish—rice, chicken, and oil—are all of Spanish origin. Still, a Cuban arroz con pollo is unmistakably Latin American. It derives its characteristic taste from the *sofrito,* a basic blend of garlic, onions, and green peppers, which lends flavor to most Cuban stews, enchilados, and soups. Another characteristic of Cuban cuisine is the *adobo,* a mixture of lime juice or bitter Seville orange juice, crushed garlic, and salt, and used to marinate most meats and poultry. Maricel Prescilla, a native of Cuba and a food consultant, advised me on the following version of this popular dish.

Platanos fritos (sautéed sweet bananas) are the classic accompaniment to this dish.

PREPARATION TIME *20 minutes*
MARINATING *2 hours minimum*
COOKING *45 minutes*

Marinade (Adobo)

2 large cloves garlic, crushed
1 teaspoon salt
Juice of 1 lime

One 4-pound chicken, cut into 8 serving pieces
2 tablespoons oil
1 medium Spanish onion, chopped
1 medium green bell pepper, seeded and chopped
1 bay leaf
1 teaspoon ground cumin
1 tablespoon sweet paprika
½ teaspoon oregano
½ teaspoon white pepper
1 cup tomato sauce
1 cup beer
2 cups rice
2 cups chicken stock
1 cup cooked green peas
2 red bell peppers, roasted and cut into strips
⅓ cup pitted, coarsely chopped green olives

1. To make marinade, mash the garlic and salt to a paste. Stir in lime juice. Rub chicken pieces with this mixture, marinating for at least 2 hours.

2. Heat 1 tablespoon oil in a large skillet with a lid, and sauté chicken pieces, skin side first, until golden brown, about 6 minutes on each side, and transfer to a plate.

3. Sauté the onion until translucent, about 3 minutes, adding oil if needed. Add green pepper and seasonings, and sauté for 2 minutes. Stir in tomato sauce and beer.

4. Add the chicken pieces, and simmer over medium heat for 5 minutes. Stir in the rice and half of the stock. Bring to a boil over medium heat. Reduce to a simmer, cover, and cook until rice is tender, about 25 minutes, adding more liquid as required.

5. Carefully mix in green peas, adjust seasoning, and arrange on a large platter. Garnish with roasted red peppers and green olives. *Serves 4.*

NORTHERN INDIA

Murgh Jhal Fareizi

Chicken in Aromatic Onion Sauce with Peppers and Tomatoes

Indian cuisine is one of intriguing flavors and captivating fragrances. It is also a personalized cuisine and depends greatly on each cook's understanding of many different herbs and spices and how each can be combined to make a highly individual dish. This recipe is an adaptation of a recipe supplied by Julie Sahni, an author and teacher of Indian cooking.

PREPARATION TIME *20 minutes*
COOKING *50 minutes*

2 whole chicken breasts, cooked, with skins removed
5 tablespoons vegetable oil
1½ cups finely chopped onions
1 teaspoon finely minced garlic
1 teaspoon ground cumin
¼ to ½ teaspoon red pepper flakes or cayenne
1 teaspoon paprika
1 teaspoon Garam Masala (page 88)
1 teaspoon powdered ginger
1 cup canned tomato purée, mixed with ½ cup water
1 large green bell pepper, seeded and cut into ½-inch slices
1 medium tomato, peeled and cut into 1-inch wedges
Lemon juice to taste
Salt to taste

1. Chop the cooked chicken breasts into quarters and set aside.
2. Heat 3 tablespoons oil in a skillet, add onions, and sauté until lightly brown, stirring constantly. Add garlic and sauté briefly. Add all the spices, stir through, then add diluted tomato purée.
3. Reduce heat to medium, and cook sauce until it has thickened and the oil begins to separate from it (about 8 to 10 minutes).
4. While the sauce is cooking, heat the remaining 2 tablespoons oil in a large skillet over high heat. Add the pepper slices, reduce heat, and cook for 2 to 3 minutes. Add the tomato slices and cooked chicken, and heat for 1 minute.
5. When ready to serve, arrange chicken, peppers, and tomatoes on a platter. Remove sauce from heat, add lemon juice and salt, and adjust seasoning. Pour hot sauce over the entire dish and serve. *Serves 4.*

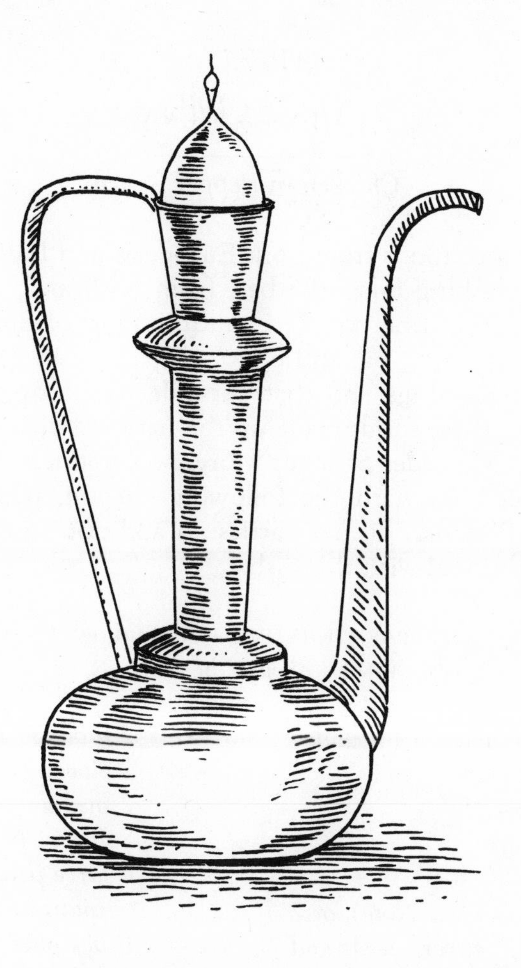

Hint

In Indian cuisine the chicken is always skinned before cooking. The reason for this practice is partly because the skin is thought to be unclean and unfit to be eaten, but in a more practical sense because the skin prevents the seasonings and flavorings from fully penetrating the meat.

PERU

Aji de Gallina

Chicken in Pepper Sauce

A blending of foods from both European and Indian cultures, Peruvian cooking takes the best from both and, so to speak, puts them all in one pot. The conquistadors of Spain contributed chicken, nuts, oil, and olives; the native Indians supplied the fiery seasonings and that versatile root crop, the potato. Combined, these foods make up the national dish of Peru—aji de gallina. Mercedes Sánchez Moreno, a frequent visitor from Peru, helped me with the following version, which is often served at Peruvian dinner parties. In addition to the potatoes, rice is traditional with this dish.

PREPARATION TIME *20 minutes*
COOKING *about 2 hours*

1 large chicken, about 5½ pounds
6 cups chicken stock
6 slices white bread
1 cup warm milk
¼ cup walnuts
1 package mirasol (see Note), or 2 dried hot red peppers, seeds and membrane removed
Achiote seeds (see Note), or 1 tablespoon heated red paprika
2 tablespoons oil
2 cloves garlic, chopped
2 medium onions, chopped
Salt and pepper to taste
6 large potatoes, cooked and quartered
Black olives for garnish
Hard-boiled eggs for garnish (optional)

1. In a 5- to 6-quart Dutch oven or stockpot, cook chicken in stock to cover for 1½ hours. Let cool in stock, then remove skin and bones, shred the meat into pieces, and set aside. (Strain stock and refrigerate or freeze for future use.)

2. Soak bread in warm milk. Crush walnuts with a rolling pin until very fine, then add to the bread mixture.

3. Heat mirasol or hot peppers in a small frying pan for about 2 minutes to bring out flavor. Add the achiote seeds or paprika and heat for a few more minutes. Add oil to obtain the desired yellow color.

4. Add garlic and onions and sauté until translucent. Add bread and walnut mixture and cook for a few minutes over moderate heat, adding more stock if necessary. Mixture should be fairly thick.

5. Adjust seasoning and transfer mixture to a large platter. Spread shredded chicken over the bread mixture, surround with potatoes, and garnish with olives. Hard-boiled eggs, cut into quarters, are part of the traditional garnish, and may also be added. *Serves 4 to 6.*

Note: Mirasol is a Peruvian pepper available only at certain ethnic markets. You can obtain an approximate flavor by using hot red peppers. *Achiote seeds* are used primarily to obtain the deep orange color typical of many Latin dishes. You can make achiote oil by combining seeds and oil in a small skillet. Heat until the oil gets to the desired color, strain, discard the seeds, and use. Bottled, it will keep indefinitely. One tablespoon red paprika, heated in oil, will produce a similar effect. Most supermarkets also carry a packaged annato seasoning product, which even the Latins find more convenient to use.

BELGIUM

Waterzooi of Chicken

Some connoisseurs claim that Belgian cuisine is even better than French. This, of course, is a matter of personal taste. What is certain is that the Belgians take food very seriously, and Belgian cuisine may well be the last bastion of classic cooking. Great care is taken with the preparation of each dish, shortcuts are frowned upon, and regular hearty meals, chock-full with good ingredients, are considered by most Belgians to be essential to a good life and disposition.

When my husband first took me to his native Belgium, I got Waterloo and waterzooi mixed up because, aside from sounding similar, I encountered both of them on the same day. Waterloo, of course, is where Napoleon suffered his final defeat, while waterzooi is Belgium's most celebrated dish. Made with either fish or chicken, waterzooi's texture lies somewhere between a soup and a stew. Made with the freshest ingredients, it has a pure and clean taste that warms stomach and heart alike.

Boiled potatoes are the usual accompaniment to this dish.

PREPARATION TIME *25 minutes*
COOKING *1 hour and 20 minutes*

2 tablespoons butter
3 celery ribs, coarsely chopped
3 large leeks, white parts only, well washed and cut into chunks
2 large onions, quartered
4 carrots, cut into large pieces
One 4- to 5-pound chicken, cut into 4 pieces
1 bouquet garni (4 sprigs of parsley, 2 bay leaves, 1 sprig of thyme, 8 peppercorns tied in cheesecloth)
5 cups chicken stock
1 cup white wine
2 egg yolks
½ cup light cream
Salt and pepper to taste
Finely chopped parsley for garnish

1. Heat the butter in a large Dutch oven or stockpot. Add the vegetables, reduce heat, and let cook for 20 minutes, without letting them brown.

2. Arrange chicken on top of the vegetables, add bouquet garni, and cover with stock and wine. Let simmer, covered, for about 45 minutes, or until chicken is tender.

3. Remove the chicken, let it cool slightly, and remove the skin and bigger bones. Place in a heated soup tureen or serving bowl.

4. Strain the stock, and discard the vegetables and bouquet garni. Return the stock to the heat and reduce liquid to 4 cups. Remove from heat.

5. Beat egg yolks and cream together in a small bowl and slowly beat this mixture into the soup. Add salt and pepper to taste and pour over chicken. Garnish with chopped parsley. *Serves 4.*

MOROCCO

Djaj M'Kalli

Chicken with Olives and Pickled Lemons

Tagines are the slowly simmered, fragrant stews that are the backbone of Moroccan cooking. The name comes from the round earthenware pot with a pointed lid in which the stews are cooked. There are unlimited variations of the savory tagine, ranging from the simplest to the most exotic. This particular tagine is one of the glories of Moroccan cuisine. In order to achieve that glory, however, the lemons must be pickled at least 3 weeks before using. But this is easily done, and the lemons keep up to a year and lend a unique flavor to lamb, vegetables, and salads.

My friend Marie Sibony, originally from Casablanca, gave me invaluable advice on the making of this exotic dish. Serve with whole-wheat pita or Moroccan bread.

PREPARATION TIME *35 minutes*
COOKING *1½ to 2 hours*

½ pound green olives
3 tablespoons vegetable oil
2 small chickens, cut into serving pieces
3 cloves garlic, crushed
2 medium onions, chopped
1 teaspoon ground turmeric
½ teaspoon ground cumin
4 to 6 saffron threads
2 Pickled Lemons (page 15)
Pinch of sugar
½ to ¾ cup chicken stock
Freshly ground pepper to taste
Chopped cilantro for garnish

1. Soak the olives in cold water, rinse, put in a pot, cover with fresh water, boil for 5 minutes to desalt completely, and rinse again. Remove pits.

2. Heat the oil in a large skillet. Sauté the chicken, a few pieces at a time to avoid crowding, until they brown. Drain fat. Add garlic, onions, olives, and seasonings.

3. Rinse the lemons, cut into strips, and add to the stew, along with some of the stock. Cover, and let simmer until the chicken is almost

coming off the bones (about 1½ to 2 hours). If more liquid is needed, add additional stock.

4. Remove the chicken, skin and debone meat if desired, and arrange in a serving dish, preferably a glazed earthenware pot. Add pepper to taste, and spoon sauce over chicken. Garnish with chopped cilantro. *Serves 4 to 6.*

MEXICO

Tortillas de Pollo con Salsa de Chile Pasilla

Tortillas with Shredded Chicken and Chile Pasilla Sauce

Mexican cuisine dates back to the early Aztec and Mayan cultures, and was based on corn, beans, tomatoes, game, or fish—peppered with hot chilies. It reached dazzling heights under Montezuma, in whose court "they prepared more than three hundred plates," according to an astonished conquistador.

The Spanish conquest of Mexico resulted in a culinary explosion that was to alter both European and Latin cuisines forever. Spain received from Mexico tomatoes, beans, vanilla, chilis, maize, chocolate, and turkey, not to mention tobacco. Native Mexicans in turn tasted their first chicken, as well as pork, wheat, rice, citrus fruits, and dairy products. They learned about Ibero-Moorish cooking procedures, combined everything, and created a flamboyant cuisine that has influenced the art of cooking worldwide.

My friend Roberta Schneiderman adapted this recipe from a dish originally featured in Diana Kennedy's *The Cuisines of Mexico*. I've made a few further changes—reducing the amount of oil, substituting a low-fat cheese for the sour cream, and skimping on the salt.

PREPARATION TIME *30 minutes*
COOKING *1 hour*

Sauce

1½ pounds tomatoes
6 chiles pasillas
¼ medium onion, peeled
¼ cup oil, preferably peanut or safflower
½ teaspoon sugar
1 teaspoon salt
1 cup Fromage Blanc (page 18)
½ cup hoop cheese, or 3 teaspoons plain low-fat yogurt mixed with ½ cup farmer's cheese, whipped until creamy

Oil
1 whole boneless and skinless chicken breast, cut into strips
12 small corn tortillas (ready-made)
1 cup grated sharp cheddar cheese
Fromage Blanc or yogurt for garnish

To make sauce:

1. Preheat broiler. Arrange tomatoes on a shallow pan and place under broiler. Broil for 20 minutes, turning them once (the resulting charred skin is thought to improve the flavor). Put tomatoes into a blender.

2. Toast the dried chilies in a preheated pan for about 15 minutes, turning them from time to time (use tongs). When cool enough to handle, remove seeds and membranes (make sure all seeds are removed, otherwise the sauce will be too hot). Add chilies and onion to blender, and blend until smooth.

3. Heat the oil in a skillet, add the blended chilies-and-tomato mixture, sugar, and salt. Cook over medium heat for about 15 minutes, stirring occasionally (if sauce splatters too much, cover). Set sauce aside to cool slightly. Combine fromage blanc and hoop cheese and stir into the sauce.*

To make tortillas:

4. Preheat the oven to 350°F.

5. Rub the bottom of a skillet with oil, and sauté chicken over high heat to sear, turning to prevent burning. Sauté for about 4 minutes. If the strips are too large, this is the time to trim them into thinner strips. Remove and fold the chicken into 1½ cups of sauce.

6. Soften tortillas according to package directions. Place a little of the chicken and sauce mixture at one end of each tortilla, roll up loosely.

7. Place the tortillas, seam side down, in an ovenproof dish. Pour the remaining sauce over them, and sprinkle with grated cheddar. Place in the preheated oven to heat through and let the cheese melt for about 10 to 15 minutes. Serve immediately. Offer a side dish of white cheese or plain yogurt to cool down the fires of the chilies. *Serves 4.*

*The sauce can be made 1 or 2 days ahead of time; in fact, the flavor improves with age. The sauce also freezes well.

Hint

Chili peppers—fresh, dried, or pickled—come in hundreds of varieties. Some are violently hot, others moderately so, some are mild. Handle a hot chili as if it were dynamite. Wear thin rubber gloves when removing the seeds and membrane, since the essence of the chili can sting your fingertips for hours after handling. Also avoid touching face or rubbing eyes when handling hot chilies.

JAPAN

Tori No Teriyaki

Chicken Teriyaki

Japanese cuisine is based on harmony among tastes, colors, shapes, and textures. The food is simply cooked to preserve its natural character, and is presented in small portions—partly necessitated by the use of chopsticks but primarily because this method helps to create an artistic presentation. I am reminded of this fact every time I eat at my favorite Japanese restaurant. Although it is a small, unpretentious New York restaurant, the cooks create mini-masterpieces that do their tradition proud. I usually sit at the counter where I can watch the cooks in action: peeling cucumbers, slicing fish, molding rice, and rolling seaweed. Not a motion is wasted; their precision is only matched by their good humor.

The food is arranged on a plain wooden block: rectangular pieces of fish or chicken, small mounds of pale ginger and wasabi, a few shreds of dark seaweed, a lacquered bowl with rice. Besides enjoying the visual beauty of the food, I experience various taste sensations: the rice is sticky, the seaweed chewy, the wasabi sharp, the ginger sour, the chicken silken. All sensory bases are touched in a Japanese meal.

As with most Japanese dishes, rice is the usual accompaniment. Spinach with sesame dressing also goes well with this selection.

PREPARATION TIME *20 minutes*
MARINATING *4 hours or overnight*
COOKING *12 minutes*

Marinade

⅓ cup soy sauce
3 tablespoons mirin or sweet sherry
1 teaspoon sugar
½ teaspoon grated fresh ginger

8 boned chicken thighs (page 11), or cut of your choice
1 tablespoon vegetable oil
Pickled ginger
Grated daikon
Thin stalks of green onion

1. Combine marinade ingredients listed on page 176. Make several slashes into both sides of the chicken and marinate chicken for 4 hours or overnight. When ready, remove chicken from marinade, drain well, and preserve marinade.

2. Heat oil in a skillet, sauté the chicken, skin side down first, until browned, about 3 minutes on either side. Add marinade sauce, cover, and cook over low heat for 6 minutes, or until chicken is done, turning the pieces once. Remove the chicken, let it cool slightly, remove skin if desired, and slice pieces at an angle into thin slices.

3. Arrange equal amounts of slices, fanlike, on each individual plate. Spoon a small amount of marinade sauce over chicken, offering the remaining sauce in separate small bowls. Garnish plates with pickled ginger, shredded daikon, and green onions. Serve with chopsticks. *Serves 4.*

Hint

Japanese rice is short-grain, polished, and unconverted. Its slight stickiness is a help when eating with chopsticks.

Bibliography

Many books and articles were consulted in the writing of this book. Those listed below were particularly helpful.

Aron, Jean-Paul. *The Art of Eating in France.* London: Peter Owen, 1975 (trans.).

Bugialli, Giuliano. *Classic Techniques of Italian Cooking.* New York: Simon & Schuster, 1982.

FitzGibbon, Theodora. *The Food of the Western World.* New York: Quadrangle, The New York Times Books, 1976.

Funk & Wagnalls. *Cooks & Diners Dictionary.* New York, 1968.

Hultman, Tami. *The Africa News Cookbook.* New York: Penguin Books, 1985.

Kennedy, Diana. *The Cuisines of Mexico.* New York: Harper & Row, 1972.

Krohn, Norman Odya. *Menu Mystique.* Middle Village, N.Y.: Jonathan David Publishers, 1983.

Leibenstein, Margaret. *The Edible Mushroom.* New York: Workman Publishing, 1986.

Montagne, Prosper. *The New Larousse Gastronomique.* New York: Crown Publishers, 1977.

Ortis, Elisabeth Lambert. *The Book of Latin American Cooking*. New York: Alfred A. Knopf, 1979.
Pépin, Jacques. *The Art of Cooking*. New York: Alfred A. Knopf, 1987.
Root, Waverley. *Food*. New York: Simon & Schuster, 1980.
Schneider, Elizabeth. *Uncommon Fruits & Vegetables*. New York: Harper & Row, 1987.
Smith, Page, and Daniel, Charles. *The Chicken Book*. San Francisco: North Point Press, 1982.
Stobart, Tom. *Herbs, Spices and Flavoring*. Woodstock, N.Y.: The Overlook Press, 1982.
Von Welanetz, Diana and Paul. *Guide to Ethnic Ingredients*. New York: Warner Books, 1982.
Witty, Helen. *Fancy Pantry*. New York: Workman Publishing, 1986.

Index